Soccer is a Thinking Game

Soccer is a Thinking Game

A Simple Approach to Coaching Youth Soccer (Ages 5-12)

Darren McKnight, PhD and Radovan Pletka

iUniverse, Inc.

New York   Bloomington   Shanghai

Soccer is a Thinking Game
A Simple Approach to Coaching Youth Soccer (Ages 5-12)

iUniverse books may be ordered through booksellers or by contacting:

iUniverse
1663 Liberty Drive
Bloomington, IN 47403
www.iuniverse.com
1-800-Authors (1-800-288-4677)

Because of the dynamic nature of the Internet, any Web addresses or links contained in this book may have changed since publication and may no longer be valid.

The views expressed in this work are solely those of the author and do not necessarily reflect the views of the publisher, and the publisher hereby disclaims any responsibility for them.

ISBN: 978-0-595-46787-7 (pbk)
ISBN: 978-0-595-91079-3 (ebk)

Printed in the United States of America

Contents

Electronic versions of selected coaches' material described in this book are available via the Web at www.cfesoccer.com.

This Web site is affiliated with the Centre For Excellence (CFE) in Fairfax, Virginia. This institution is committed to bring high-caliber, innovative soccer training to northern Virginia and southern Maryland. Its staff and programs, while focused on local youth, are active in global outreach and collaborative efforts that fuel excellence in soccer.

A set of advanced visual teaching aids, called Thinkables™, is available through the CFE Web site. This material takes the concept of *Soccer Is a Thinking Game* to the next level of sophistication. Just as with this book, the Thinkables™ aids are presented in age-appropriate groups. They bring all of the lessons in this book to life visually and provide a means to advance your team's collective and individual skills. Since the Thinkables™ are in digital form, you can customize them and print them for your team.

Acknowledgments

I would like to thank all of the soccer coaches who have been so patient with me while I have tried to master soccer and learn to coach this beautiful sport. They have all forgotten more about soccer than I will ever know: Phill Brummett, Chris Mustain, Jon Holl, Debbie Berg, John Utley, Larry Taylor, Bob Zarnich, Sean Fitzsimmons, Karen Fiala, Dean Kemp, Sue Hicks, Jessica Lawless, Rado Pletka (my coauthor), Tamir Linhart, Cara Patton, Nadir Moumen, Brian Cummins, Rich Gleason, Hamisi Amani-Dove, Dan Ayoub, John Collins, and many more whom I have probably left out. To those I have omitted, I apologize. I would also like to thank the Chantilly Youth Association (CYA), my daughters' team's host soccer club, for giving me the opportunity to coach youth sports.

I want to thank the girls whom I have coached over the years, who have been so patient with my lack of soccer experience, receptive to my non-traditional coaching techniques, and amazingly capable at grasping the subtleties of this elegant sport at such a young age.

Last, I want to thank my family for indulging my love of science and my never-ending belief that everything in life is related. I constantly tell them that if they are kind, honest, and do your best, then everything will work out well in life. For the constant "experimentation" of my attempted insights into soccer and other parts of life, my daughters, Grace and Olivia, have been especially forgiving. It is never fun to be the coach's daughter, and they have weathered the extra attention with humor and dignity. Thanks for being such good sports. My wife, Alison, has been incredibly kind as I have immersed myself into coaching a soccer team, a basketball team, a track squad, or writing this book. I guess I am that third child we never realized we had. Thanks for being supportive and understanding!

—*Darren McKnight*

I strongly believe in the relation between team sports and life lessons, especially in the game of soccer. As I have matured in life, I have found that I have become a better person in all facets of my life due to the game of soccer. It has taught me the importance of communications, respect, hard work, dedication, sacrifice, and tolerance. Moreover, being part of a team, as well as traveling for games, gave me the opportunity to mingle with many different people of all races, backgrounds, and culture. This soccer journey has been priceless.

So many people have helped me and been a part of this trek, and I am forever thankful and grateful. I would first like to thank Tamir Linhart for giving me my first opportunity to start working with youth soccer many years ago. I would like to extend a special thanks to Larry Paul for being a constant mentor to me, and all the coaches, especially Joe Soos (Lake Braddock High School), Avieris (Greece), and my former manager, Thanasis (Greece), who have helped me so much.

I also want to thank all the boys and girls whom that I have had the opportunity and pleasure of training and coaching. It has been a joy to watch as most of these players have matured and gone on to play at a higher level. Many thanks also go to my family, and most important, my fiancé, Lili, who has had to put up with my passion for soccer. I greatly appreciate her understanding of my busy training schedule.

Special thanks also go to the Toobin family who have been there for me and provided me with so much for so many years, as well as my dear Fornecker family.

Last, but certainly not least, many thanks go to all my teammates, who have had to put up with me and with whom I have enjoyed the pleasure of being on a team over the years (you as well, Yinz). Thank you!

—*Radovan Pletka*

Darren McKnight, PhD and Radovan Pletka

The authors would like to thank Derek McCleskey, Sean Fitzsimmons, April Dougherty, and Stevie Alibi for the photographs in this book. Derek and Sean have tirelessly captured pictures of our soccer teams for years. A special thanks to these two for their long-term commitment to recording the excitement of this wonderful sport.

Introduction

I love to teach and learn; I have been doing one or the other—or both—my entire life, and I hope that I will teach and learn the rest of my life. As an engineer and scientist, I have applied the scientific method countless times and have become comfortable with it in every facet of my life. The scientific method (observation, hypothesis building, experimentation, and drawing conclusions) is a wonderful cycle that I have internalized over the years. I learned in my industry career that when I was challenged with trying to navigate through a new domain, I simply conducted research and asked experienced people in that community for help.

When we were challenged with office buildings contaminated with *bacillus anthracis* bacterium (often called anthrax), I looked at applying an electrostatic spray mechanism, similar to that found in automobile painting shops, for depositing liquid decontaminants to clean up the exposed surfaces. Testing and experimentation brought this concept into operational use in a short period of time. Similarly, when examining inconsistencies in the number of fragments produced when satellites exploded in space, I initiated an experimental program that culminated in the hypervelocity impact testing of a Navy satellite in a ground test facility to produce much more accurate models for all on-orbit collision events. The common theme in both of these workplace examples and the creation of this book is that I observed a problem, hypothesized how to solve it, experimented with components of the solution, and then developed the solution.

When my older daughter, Olivia, asked me to help coach her soccer team, I struggled to find a youth soccer coaching book that addressed the relevant issues. Apparently, all of the other parents were in the same situation as I was, so they were not much help. The coaches I knew were buying coaching manuals that showed hundreds of drills using tens of cones and lots of complicated soccer terms. There was very little discussion of what the players did without the ball and even less about what coaches did when not on the field.

As I started to think about what made sense to help the children have fun and to manage the expectations of the parents, I needed to apply many skills that I had routinely used in my work environment, such as organization, communications, planning, and innovation, powered by the application of the scientific method. None of these topics are covered in other youth soccer coaching books. I also started to make up new drills, handouts, games, and rituals that seemed to help my young players improve and have fun. As I started to write these down and assemble them so that I could more easily reuse them, I had the pleasure of meeting Radovan Pletka, my coauthor.

Radovan is a true soccer enthusiast and a scholar of the sport. Rado has an amazing legacy of success related to soccer equaled only by the infectious enthusiasm that he brings to the soccer field as a professional trainer. He has played and trained soccer at very high levels nearly his entire life, playing competitively on three continents and earning several top player honors throughout the years. Yet, he remarked that the approach that I was applying was different than he had ever seen. However, he believed that my methodologies for teaching and engaging with youth soccer players could indeed be a powerful enabler for coaching soccer not just for young players, but at many levels.

At that time, we decided to merge my pragmatic, yet innovative, outlook with Rado's skilled and practical knowledge of soccer to create *Soccer Is a Thinking Game* to help parents around the world who want to coach their children in youth soccer but have not believed they could handle it.

This book is different from any other soccer book. Other books tell you that ballhandling skills are the most important aspect of youth soccer. We do not agree. Thinking is the most important activity for the youth soccer player, and positioning is the most important measurable performance resulting from thinking. Ballhandling skills are naturally an individual attribute, whereas positioning is more of a team attribute, since this performance is always based upon where a player's teammates are.

Players with exceptional ballhandling skills can easily lose confidence as they get frustrated at not being able to use their skills correctly, because they are not in the right place on the field to fully exploit those skills or are not thinking about how, when, and where to use those skills. If a player is not in the right place on the soccer field, he will need much more stamina and much better ballhandling skills to cover for the poor positioning. Positioning is the epitome of teamwork. Being where the team needs the player the most is critical to playing quality soccer.

As your players progress, ballhandling skills become more and more important. However, by focusing on thinking and positioning in the early years, players coached this way will be better team players and also more productive as individual players. The bottom line is that decision-making will differentiate the good soccer player from the great soccer player, and this book provides the best instruction for teaching solid decision-making skills.

We hope that this book serves you well as a guide to make the youth soccer experience a positive one that leads to many fun family moments. It will serve create a foundation for advanced soccer play by children throughout their lives.

How to Use This Book

As with any training aid, you will need some guidance as to how to best apply the information in this book. We have reviewed each chapter below with our thoughts about what each provides the youth soccer coach so that you can most efficiently focus on what you need to read and review.

Chapter 1, "Ten Keys to Soccer Coaching," is a summary of the entire book and discusses a variety of topics. Every coach should read this section, but the first-year coach will only use about half of the material discussed. Read it anyway, to see where you will be going in the years to come.

Chapter 2, "Teaching Is the Key," provides critical insights into how a coach should talk to his players and their parents. This is a useful chapter for all coaches because other soccer coaching books usually do not include this topic. We think it is the most important chapter in the book, since it explains the effective means for providing and using all the other information presented later in the book. It is also important because the young soccer player is just a child who needs to be spoken to in positive, encouraging ways. At the same time, your communication needs to be focused, and you must use visual techniques to maximize the enjoyment, success, and satisfaction for the players and the parents.

Chapter 3, "Season Milestones," covers when the coach needs to do certain tasks throughout the course of a season. This chapter helps you get organized and reviews many aspects of a typical soccer season, such as practices, games, team logistics, social activities, and motivational techniques. The Game Day section includes hints about how to prepare yourself and your team for the match each weekend.

Chapter 4, "Basics of Soccer," provides useful material about soccer rules and standards. The information here is essential for your role as a youth soccer coach; however, it is not intended to be an exhaustive source of all soccer terms. We have paid special attention to include items that are generally misunderstood in youth soccer in the hope that we can save you and your team some troubles during the season.

Chapter 5, "Drills and Positioning," covers specific, age-appropriate activities to perform in practice and as warm-ups before games. This chapter focuses on tasks that keep the players active with the ball and includes a manageable number of new skills to teach each season. A unique cumulative approach to drills provides a robust set of activities for use in practice that result in high efficiency. The Formations section provides insight into how to arrange your players on the field.

Chapter 6, "Moving to Travel Soccer," discusses when you need to start to turn over more and more of the coaching and training of the team to a professional. This book assumes that the coach has played little or no soccer. It is possible to be a fantastic youth soccer coach with limited experience in playing soccer. However, as your players make the move to travel soccer this is no longer true. You will need help, and the players on your team must have augmented training and coaching from individuals who are experienced in playing and training soccer players.

What Is Next?

Now let's get started with the ten overarching elements of soccer coaching. Write these principles down and internalize them early in your coaching career. They will serve as a valuable support structure through the years.

CHAPTER 1

Ten Keys to Soccer Coaching

The following "Ten Keys to Soccer Coaching" will be reinforced with drills, positioning schemes, handouts, seasonal activities, and more throughout this book. Some of them, however, may run counter to common soccer coaching sentiment. This is because we think of soccer not only as a sport, but also an essential part of the development of a young person. Just as reading, writing, and arithmetic are considered essential aspects of early intellectual activity, the attributes that we wish to instill in young soccer players—such as mutual respect, good decision making, and discipline—are essential to the early social development of young people.

While these factors are important to the social development of children, the proper execution of these techniques also will result in wildly successful soccer teams and expert individual play. That is the interesting reality that we have observed over the years of coaching: the less you worry about winning, the more you win! The more you focus on the team, the more the individuals get out of the experience.

Remember that these rules are reinforced throughout the book with very specific actions that you as a coach can take. The first five keys are more general and could apply to any sport. In fact, I have used these tips for basketball and track very successfully. The last five rules are specific to soccer and are appropriate for all ages, but they are applied differently for each age group.

These ten rules establish recurring themes found throughout this book. Some may seem hard to apply at first, but after a few seasons, they will come naturally and, in turn, the success of your team will come naturally. This book and these rules are not about immediate success but rather about building a strong foundation upon which an excellent team can take root and give rise to great individual players with fantastic skills and an understanding of soccer as a sport.

General Keys: Simple but Not Easy

1. Multiply by subtracting; keep it simple.

Take the complexities out of the coaching process, and you will see increased understanding, development, and motivation. Over the years, I have found that teaching three new items at a time is the maximum that can be done reliably. This worked in my physics class, with my children at home, and on the soccer field.

A landmark paper by George Miller, "The Magical Number Seven, Plus or Minus Two," published in *Psychological Review* in 1956, demonstrated that most people could only remember between five to nine simple items. For more complex items, people could remember fewer. Additionally, Dr. Miller and others have discussed the process of chunking information into groups of three to aid in being able to remember more information, more quickly. This widely referenced academic research reinforces my classroom and field experience.

Be consistent and use repetition. Pick three skills that you want your team to master, then work on those three skills all season. Be consistent with drills at practice for the skills to become habits with the players and the team as a whole. Reinforce them at practice, in games, and after games. Talk about them; draw pictures that represent them. Be creative but be consistent. Focus on what is important, and then have your players do it over, and over, and over until they get it right.

Play to their strengths while improving their weaknesses. Limit the cones used in practice. Do you see any cones on the field during a game? Too many cones take away from what the children should focus on. The children start worrying too much about what each different cone means and focus too much on trying to get to the right cone instead of focusing on what they are supposed to do with or without the ball. In other words, they forget about the drill itself.

Even as your players get older and more skilled, resist the temptation to introduce too many skills and drills each season. The ability to perform a few skills very well is always better than knowing how to do fifty skills poorly.

2. Be visual.

Write everything down, and use pictures and physical props whenever you can. Many children (and adults) learn much better with pictures. This is where good soccer players becoming coaches can possibly be at a disadvantage, because they understand all aspects of soccer intuitively. They do not recall a time when a skill was introduced and they did not understand it.

Soccer skills must be built up one by one with pictures, diagrams, and photos to help the novice soccer player learn. Think about how children learn to add and subtract. They use visual aids; they are not given endless mathematical problems when they are first introduced to new math concepts. Often, the use of coins, pieces of candy, and toothpicks supplement lessons teaching addition and subtraction. Similarly, coaches can use videotapes of games, diagrams of plays, and even toy figurines to help explain important teaching points.

3. Soccer is a thinking game.

No matter how many elite soccer coaches have tried to convince me that individual ballhandling skills are the first key component for a developing player to master, the real soccer minds know that soccer is 80 percent mental. When children are first learning to play soccer, it is important to discuss where each player should be on the field. So it is your job to create thinking players by the way you interact with your players (ask them what they think), by giving out handouts as assignments (exercise their understanding of the game off the field), and by teaching visualization to your players early (visualizing doing a skill properly is almost as effective as actually doing the drill).

Once your players know where they need to be on the field and what they need to do, then—and only then—can the ball handling skills help them. What good is it to have great ballhandling skills if the player has no idea how to really apply them?

It is also important to let your players make mistakes, since we all learn more from mistakes than from successes. Mistakes help children see earlier what the ramifications are for doing something wrong, and they help players refine their on-field decision making. More important, the kids will remember being beaten by the other team more than if the coach continually places each player in the right location. Without making mistakes, by the time they get older, they would have learned nothing and not improved much because they were so used to someone else telling them what to do and how to do it in games.

For example, if you take a look at children in sports, most of the accomplished ones have parents or siblings whom they have watched perform in sports and seen the importance of really knowing the game, not just playing it. The sooner players understand that greater knowledge will permit them to make better decisions, the sooner they will become expert players.

4. Soccer is a microcosm of life.

Soccer teaches important life lessons, such as working together as a team is more important than individual skills; always do your best; lead by example; and the less you worry about winning the more you win. We focus on all these lessons in this book.

For youth soccer, the focus should be on learning and understanding how to play the sport the right way. Children actually enjoy it when they do things correctly. They want someone to be proud of them. It is all about *how* you teach them, not just *what* you teach them.

This book will show you when there is an opportunity to teach a life lesson critical for soccer, but more important, a lesson for life off the field. For example, one key to life is to trust your colleagues and friends. This principle relates to soccer being a thinking game. A common line that we use is: "Trust your teammates and be a team player. There are no stars on this team." Stars will eventually be born, but only out of hard work and not by what anyone on the outside sees.

As a youth soccer coach, it is important to lead by example. Never ask kids to do anything that you do not do. Run with them, do the drills, etc. Players look up to their coaches, especially at such a young age. Tell the kids about a weakness that you have, and let them see you work on it at every practice. It can be related to soccer, but does not have to be. Make a habit of talking about it and having discussions about your progress.

Teach them the right way to play and how you expect them to play. However, you must also allow them the room for mistakes. Let them know it is okay to make mistakes, as long as they know what they did wrong. Lack of freedom to make mistakes will stunt their creative and imaginative growth, just like in life. Coach *on* the bench, not *from* the bench. In work terminology, do not micro-manage your team.

5. Use only results-driven drills.

To get the most intensity and focus out of any drill, you must identify an objective for it. Do not just set up cones and order players to do drills. Add an element of tolerable, low-pressure competitiveness to the drills. For example, give points to the team or individual with the most accurate passes, timed drills, or most skills used in a particular scenario. Then, reward the winning group. Perhaps excuse those players from picking up cones after practice, or let them select what the coach does after the drill (such as pushups or laps).

Always keep the ball at the feet of the kids. Do not have them stand in line, especially the younger players. Any drill you conduct should be related to the three skills you are teaching for the season, as stated in the first rule. Make the drills realistic and game-like. In other words, play a lot of soccer. If you practice with a result in mind, it is more likely you will achieve it.

Soccer-Specific Keys: Play Hard, Play Smart

6. What you do without the ball is more important than what you do with the ball.

Players often overlook this insight until they get into their teens, but it is the most important rule for beginning soccer players. It will improve the cohesive-ness of your team because it reinforces that everyone is contributing to the suc-cess of the team. Success is not based on the child who is scoring. The rule also enables your players to increase their confidence by putting them in the right place. As a result, players are usually required only to make an average play to help the team, whereas if they are out of position, they will often have to make a great play to contribute.

As we will discuss later, soccer (like most team sports played on a field) is all about creating and denying space on the field. This is normally done when players do not have the ball but anticipate getting the ball.

7. Run in straight lines.

The youth soccer game is often jokingly called magnet ball, as all of the players just follow the ball around the field. The typical peewee soccer game looks more like a session of follow the leader than a soccer match. The kids really mean well; they want to get to the ball and just have a chance to kick it. Unfortunately, they normally do not care where they kick it. Many peewee players are just as happy kicking it into their own goal as they are kicking it into an opponent's goal. This does not need to be the case!

Your players must know where they need to go and then go there. As you know, the shortest distance between two points is a straight line. Your players should have the confidence to know why they are running forward, running laterally, attacking, or passing, etc., so that they do their task, then move on to the next task.

While seemingly all about physical actions, running in straight lines is more about positioning and decision making. Players must run to where they need to be, then react to the next set of events—which may, in turn, result in going in yet another direction. However, your players must anticipate where the ball or the opponents are going, then get there quickly, hopefully first.

8. Keep your head up and eyes on the ball.

If your player cannot see the ball, the field, or the other players, how can he do the right thing? This is true for every age group, but for each age group you apply this rule in different ways.

For peewees, you just want them to actually watch the ball (versus the cute puppy on the sidelines or a pretty yellow flower) without any great intent. As long as they know when the ball is coming their way or going the opposite direction, they will be able to interact and start to learn.

By the time you coach tweens (ten to twelve-year-olds), watching the ball is not so simple. Watching the ball is all about anticipating what it will do next, how the other team will respond to the ball, how teammates will react to the flow of the ball, and will the ball bounce twice or three times, for instance.

Keeping the head up is not just about the ball. It is about the location of teammates, where the other team is positioned, and if there is an open space to the left or to the right. If a player's head is not up, he probably is not taking in the proper information to make the best decision.

Anthony is dribbling the ball but looking upfield, figuring out where his teammates and opponents are positioned.

9. Attack the ball.

A coach must strive to get their players to *want* the ball. Whether it is in the air, on the ground, or with an opponent, you must encourage your kids that the closest player to the ball from your team should be the first one from either team to get to it. Teach your players that any ball in the air, rolling, or being dribbled by an opponent is *theirs* to get. It is important to remind your players, however, that they should never take the ball from a teammate.

The game does not change while the ball is traveling in the air or on the ground. Only when it reaches its next destination is when the game can change, so you must emphasize to your players that they must be that destination. Anytime the ball goes from one player to another, the game situation changes drastically. Therefore, if your player can win the ball directly from an opponent, then the game is greatly simplified in your team's favor. Winning the ball is an opportunity for you to teach your players that they can accumulate small victories in a well played game.

The aggressiveness and confidence to think of that ball as theirs will take time to nurture, but without that urgency, your team will fail. I remember winning games by a large margin and the only difference was the aggressiveness of our team at getting to the loose ball first. The difference may be the time between a player letting a ball roll to him versus sprinting to the ball. The difference may be the greater anticipation gained by hundreds of repetitions of trapping drills. No matter how they acquire it, your team must display this aggressiveness in order to improve and be successful.

10. Keep your hips over the ball.

Young players often are afraid of getting their body into the play and have a tendency to want to poke at the ball with their foot. When you ask your players why they are standing away from the ball and trying to poke and prod at it, they usually say that they are trying to avoid getting hurt or run into.

The opposite is actually true. If they get their body over the ball, when shooting, tackling, dribbling, or possessing the ball, they are much less likely to get hurt. First, their balance will be better if both feet are on the ground and their knees are bent. If they are poking at the ball, this usually means that one foot is off the ground and the other leg is probably straight. This is the least sturdy stance. With their leg extended, it is also more likely that another fast-moving player can come by and run into them in such a way as to cause them to get a twisted knee or ankle. If your players keep their hips over the ball, it will also deter other players from going after it or cause them to just poke at it.

Three Components of Success

The total impact of these ten rules is to produce a framework that starts with *parental support*. You strengthen this foundation by reinforcing the *thinking aspect* of playing soccer. Finally, you polish it by the thoughtful execution of a few *quality drills* to enhance individual and team skills. These three components reinforce and support each other; you will not have a good player or good team without all three.

Parental support is critical for simple logistics, such as getting their child to your practice and games reliably on time. However, parental support is even more important for reinforcing the life lessons of soccer. You must remember that for most preteen kids, soccer is good, clean fun but is (probably) not a stepping-stone to realizing Olympic soccer dreams.

Win or lose, parents need to understand your concept of team and individual skills to make your job easier as a coach and to maximize the amount their child learns. What a child learns normally determines how much they like soccer. Teaching soccer is not about how much your team wins, but rather how much your players learn. You do need to occasionally win some games to keep up the players' confidence and the enthusiasm, but winning need not be the focus of all activities.

Talk to any team that wins a championship several years in a row (without any challenge) and ask the players if they are having fun. They probably are not having fun or improving since they are not being challenged. This situation makes it unlikely that they will learn any of the life lessons from soccer. Everyone must get a little out of their comfort zone in order to improve and advance. In soccer, this is done by entering tournaments with tougher and tougher competition when league play is no longer demanding enough.

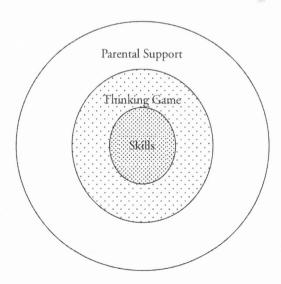

Parental support reinforces the thinking part of soccer, which is based on mastering a few essential soccer skills through results-driven drills.

Almost all of the ten keys to coaching soccer reinforce the second major aspect of this sport, which is thinking. Our emphasis on this aspect is a big difference between this and other soccer coaching books. Other books focus on ballhandling skills first, and then have you evolve the thinking aspect of the game for when the players are older. However, we believe that you make better soccer players, better young people, and better teams by emphasizing the need for players to think and make decisions on the field from the first time they take the field. It is critical for young people to manage a variety of demands on their time and attention in school, at play, and on the soccer field.

Coaching youth soccer is all about balance. You should work to advance all aspects of soccer—thinking, ballhandling, positioning—together at the same time.

The soccer field might be the first place where kids will be able to process the "see a problem, come up with a solution, and see the results" sequence. They will go through this type of process countless times as they grow up and when they are adults. Thinking about soccer can help develop their capabilities to cope with situations on the field and of the field. Getting your players to think doesn't necessarily mean having them handle complex situations, but rather getting them at a young age to understand the need and importance of figuring out ways to solve simple problems.

The last of the three elements of our soccer framework that these ten rules support is skills. Even this aspect of the book is different from others. We present very few drills relative to a standard youth soccer coaching book because we believe it is more important to master a few basic skills and then apply them creatively in decision-making situations, both in practice and in games.

Stages of Youth Soccer

We have broken down the seven years of youth soccer into three age groups, which we use to organize material later in the book. Below we describe the groups and offer some high-level objectives for each:

-       Peewee (five to seven years old): Make it fun, and strive for every child to play for several seasons. You cannot tell when a child is seven years of age if soccer is or is not his sport. Therefore, you must make it fun and rewarding for everyone. Relating to such young kids requires paying special attention to how and what you say. You must have energy and humor; correct players only on safety and discipline issues.

- Middle years (seven to nine years old): Make improvements as a team first, then as individuals. At this age, it starts to become clear which children are natural soccer players, but you also notice the kids whose work ethic and intelligence will enable them to be excellent players. You must reinforce *the team* over *the individual* in this age group. You also must manage the expectations of the parents. You do not know if their child will ever play in the Olympics, but you are sure that they will improve, as long as they play hard and play smart.

- Tween years (nine to twelve years old): Individual skills start to emerge in comparison with team skills. Individual kids start to mature earlier and focus on a single sport. These children start to distance themselves from the others. Integrating the exceptional kids into the team dynamic, which might include many mediocre players, is a critical job of the coach. This is also the time when many soccer clubs start to offer travel or elite squads to provide opportunities for players of all skill levels to be challenged and have fun. We include more on travel soccer in chapter six.

What Is Next?

Players must practice the basic skills and drills provided in this book over and over in order to master them, but we will provide just a few so that the overall process is not too daunting. As we have said before, keep it simple. All of the drills shown in this book are ones you can build upon over time, thus simplifying both your preparation and the practices for your players. You can make these activities more difficult incrementally to continue to challenge your players as they advance and to match the skills needed for more precise, tactically oriented soccer as your players get older. As you look at each drill in this book, you realize that each is designed in a way so that you can build upon it to make it more complex as your team gets older and better. Or, you can subtract certain elements to simplify the drill.

The next chapter discusses teaching. It is the means by which we, as coaches, impart knowledge, insights, advice, and confidence to our players and their parents.

CHAPTER 2

Teaching Foundations

~~Coaching~~ → Teaching

Your role as a soccer coach is all about teaching first, not coaching. Do it right, and be consistent from season to season. Explain what you will be doing, and how you will be doing it. Listen to assistant coaches, parents, and other coaches, but make changes slowly and deliberately.

Other parents and other players may talk about their soccer program and how good it is. Make it clear that your team has its own personality and plan. Be patient and focus on the ten keys of soccer. Do not focus on winning. Focus on what is important to your team, to you, and to your parents, and always make your focus a positive objective that you have control over. You do not have control over winning (more on this later).

Teach parents

It is important to teach parents, as well as the players, what to expect from your soccer program. Parents need to learn about the fundamentals of soccer, your expectations of discipline on the field, how you will run practice, and many other items that you will be learning about in this book. Parents can even end up serving as assistants on and off the field if they know what you have in mind for the team.

Communicate to them. If you all have the same objective, and if you have defined the steps that each of you can take to attain that objective, then you will all contribute to the success of the team.

Do you "get it"?

So many soccer coaches have played soccer. However, we believe that for coaching youth soccer, having extensive soccer experience might make it harder to be a good coach. How can it be bad to know how to play soccer well? The problem is that five-to twelve-year-olds may never have played soccer before, so the concepts of dribbling, passing, tackling, juggling, volleying, for instance, are all new to them. If you have played soccer for years, it is hard to remember what it was like to not understand how to dribble the ball. You have always "gotten it," for as long as you can remember.

Being a scientist, who played a little intramural soccer as a professor at the Air Force Academy, I definitely did not "get it" when it came to playing soccer. So when I started to coach peewee soccer, it was as new to me as it was to my five-year-old daughter. As a result, I came up with some non-traditional approaches to coaching peewee soccer players to make it more intuitive for the typical five-year-old. Those early interactions were the genesis for this book.

Many soccer books talk about defensive pressure and filling the lanes; but these concepts and others are too advanced for peewee players, so we came up with a simple imaginary line concept for inspiring some early offensive and defensive skills. We developed this concept of an imaginary line between the ball and the goal to introduce the idea of creating and denying space in terms relevant to a five-year-old. We developed and included several other similar, unique approaches that were borne out of an attempt to break down the concept of offense and defense into an engineering problem (since I did not know any better).

The power of threes

Use the power of threes: three key skills each season, three areas each practice, three skills for each position. This is a small enough number of items that you can remember. We will talk more about this in the next chapter.

Keep it simple

No matter what age group, what you teach must be simple, even if it is not easy. Soccer is a simple game: kick the ball down the field. It is critical to not overwhelm the players on your team with complex terms and complicated drills. You must balance challenging the kids without deflating their confidence.

Boys vs. girls

This balance is even more tenuous because girls and boys really are different and need to be coached differently. The mantra that we embrace is that "boys lack focus, girls lack confidence." The way in which you communicate, challenge, and reward your team will depend on both their age and their gender. It is more likely that boys will respond well to challenging drills that they cannot do very well and to competitions in practice where the loser has to do a lap. Girls need to have skills introduced a bit more slowly. They are still very competitive, but early on, having competitions where winners and losers are identified is not productive. By the time they are tweens, girls can handle this type of competition better.

Boys seem to care more about winning than girls. However, girls are normally more attentive, so they will improve faster because they generally learn faster and better. Of course, these observations are generalities that may or may not be true depending on the group of kids on your team. The important fact to remember is that children are different, and you need to be attentive to how they respond to you. Tailor your approach for the personality, strengths, and weaknesses of your team.

Teaching Fundamentals

For either gender, it is critical to have four teaching fundamentals in place.

First, keep teaching points to one to two minutes at a time and get down to their level physically (e.g., kneel down or "take a knee"). Keep your comments to less than one minute once practice begins to keep up the continuity and interest from the kids. This also contributes to conditioning by insuring that your players do not stand around too much. Instruction is more productive if given while they are doing the activity rather than when they are standing around getting distracted by their teammates or siblings and parents on the sidelines.

Second, select drills that keep the ball on the kids' feet, as much as possible. Avoid drills where the kids are standing in line, especially in the peewee and middle years.

Third, do not use any words in your teaching interactions that require an explanation. Use their vocabulary, along with pictures and diagrams.

Fourth, teach three items in each practice, game, or season. Do not try to do too much, and make sure that your efforts are cumulative.

Repetition: practice makes permanent (not perfect)

You should think about teaching/coaching just like these kids learn math in school. They learn basic techniques (e.g., adding) and then they practice, practice, practice until what seemed difficult comes easily, almost without thinking. Next, they learn the opposite of adding: subtracting. They practice, practice, practice until they can add and subtract almost by instinct. Any bad habits that they learn early they get very good at doing incorrectly over and over again. It is critical to understand that "practice makes permanent, not perfect." Soccer coaches often neglect this fact. What kids learn at this age will be difficult for them to unlearn later. For that reason, we suggest drills and exercises very early that focus on using both feet and looking up when dribbling, for example.

Having the tendency to kick with only one foot or constantly looking at the ground when dribbling are two bad habits that are tough to break, but these skills (dribbling with both feet and dribbling with the head up) are very important to being productive in the tween years.

You have heard the adage "pay me now or pay me later." This is relevant in coaching soccer. Build a foundation of solid soccer understanding and skills early on. This will pay off in later years, when you will not have to spend time reteaching the players to perform a skill the correct way.

Be careful with hands-on coaching

As an adult, who your players' parents have entrusted their children for several hours a week, you have a responsibility to act respectfully to their children. This involves not being either too tough or too nice. You should never touch your players harshly or in anger. Similarly, you need to be careful to commend your players mostly by kind words. High fives and "knuckle taps" are safe. Just imagine how you would like your child to be treated by another adult in the same situation, and you undoubtedly will act appropriately. Male coaches of girl teams must be especially careful.

All leagues have very specific rules about this aspect of your interaction with your team. Suffice it to say that you must follow the rules of your league, at a minimum.

Preparing for practice

What you do before and after practices and games is just as important as what you do during practices and games. The similarity between this statement and the axiom "what you do without the ball is more important than what you do with the ball" is purposeful and instructive.

If you do not get down on one knee and ask the kids how their weekend or school was when they get to practice, then why would you expect them to work hard and listen to you during practice? These interactions provide you the opportunity to learn about activities they are performing at school or at home that might be relevant. For instance, if the kids are preparing projects for a science fair, you might weave that into your discussions by asking the kids, "What do you think my hypothesis is about passing?" They will discuss the "if, then, therefore" chain, which is very applicable to learning soccer, so you can use their current interest in this terminology to pose your practice objectives in a way that catches their attention.

After practice

After practice, you can pick up a couple of their soccer backpacks and say that you know that they are tired so you are offering up some help. They may say, "We are not tired, coach" which either means they are not tired (and you could have worked them a bit harder) or they are just polite. Ask them what part of the practice they liked the best. Make sure that you tell the parents of the kids who did not stay for practice how well their child did in practice. Children love to hear their parents being told how good they are!

Observe which children have parents who are effusive with their praise and which ones are more critical. You may have to remind the critical parents to be more supportive.

Self-fulfilling prophecy

Expect a lot and you will get a lot. Expect little and you will get little.

This does not mean pushing the kids too hard. It means exerting steady but reasonable pressure to improve while giving the kids the benefit of the doubt as to their capacity each day to work hard. As long as they know that you are listening to them and care about them, it will make them work harder. The moment a child feels you either do not care or do not have their best interest in mind, he will stop working hard.

Your expectations should be based upon how well you know your players and the overall makeup of the team. A youth's ability and motivation are heavily affected by factors outside of learning and playing of soccer. Some kids play soccer because of friends or their parents. Early on, few children are there because they really love soccer. It is your job to encourage, teach, and inspire them to love exercise, competition, soccer, and the opportunities to learn life lessons on the soccer field.

Be positive

Make practice fun. Many times you will run a drill that goes well, and other times the same drill doesn't go well, yet the kids enjoy it. You can make practice fun in two ways. First, your attitude makes a huge difference. If you are upbeat and positive, the kids also will be enthusiastic and energetic. Second, the drill itself is critical, so select each one carefully and with your team's personality in mind. Some drills are just intrinsically more fun or challenging than others. For some drills, the players get to shoot or are active in some other way. However, how you interact with the kids makes a big difference in how much fun they have, regardless of the drill. Be positive, be creative in your praise, and move around. Your players will be no more active or enthusiastic than you are.

Think of ten ways to say "good job." Do not just say "good job" over and over again. Try to be more creative, such as "Excellent," "Superb," "Fantastic,"

"Amazing," "Great," "Wow," and "Well done." (Seriously, write down ten ways to say "good job" in the spaces below and then use them in practice and games.)

1.
2.
3.
4.
5.
6.
7.
8.
9.
10.

Communicate

Being able to communicate to your players, parents, and other coaches is critical. Throughout this book, we emphasize many techniques to help you be a better communicator and ensure that you make your points clear to both your players and their parents. As shown below, communications is the foundation that builds trust and understanding between people and permits our ability to cooperate. Cooperation entails activities that lead to a shared vision for your team, which then provides the framework for a truly collaborative and innovative team. This is where you want your team to be. They should be confident of their own decision-making skills on the field and be innovative about how they respond to situations on the field.

Communications is the beginning of the innovation sequence shown below, which you want to see applied on the soccer field.

Communications → *trust*

then

cooperation → *shared vision*

then

collaboration → *innovation (better decision making on the field)*

This sequence, while created for the scientific world, is applicable to your job as a coach. You must communicate early and often with players and parents. Be specific. Send e-mails, make phone calls, and/or give handouts. These should cover items such as your expectations for getting kids to practice and games and what they should expect in practice and games.

However, the most important aspect of communications is to listen. If you just talk, the parents and kids may nod their heads and you will think that everyone is in agreement. However, if you do not hear them repeat back your words accurately, then you probably are not getting your message across. That means that your message is too complex, they really do not want to do it your way, or you have not repeated your message enough.

What do the parents and kids want out of soccer: Olympic greatness, free babysitting, exercise, to learn soccer, enhanced competition, to improve sportsmanship, or enjoy an active social hour? You really need to listen and understand what parents and kids want from you. You will spend the majority of your time dealing with discord in the ranks if you do not focus on getting to the cooperation phase as soon as possible.

Once there is a clear understanding of what you expect and the kids and parents expect, you all can start to cooperate. Cooperation will permit you to focus on soccer and not worry about getting kids to practice on time, or what positions they are playing, or if your team is winning enough games.

Cooperation provides the foundation for your team to start to learn, and learning is the most critical aspect of collaboration. When your players are learning, then you know that your team will start to improve. You should emphasize getting your players and parents to put all of their effort into getting better and enjoying soccer. The essence of soccer excellence is quality decision-making on the field under any circumstance (i.e., real-time innovation).

Words to avoid and words to use

You should avoid using certain words when teaching/coaching youth.

Never. If you use the word *never*, you are telling your players that a certain action is always correct or incorrect, but that is hardly ever true. You build a good player by providing a graduated appreciation for soccer. In early soccer years, the best thing to do is usually quite clear, but as the skill level rises of the players, the options increase drastically for kids. So you can say *never* to the peewee players, but then you will have to reteach them in the next stage. For instance, in peewee we teach players to respond to the ball and the goal with little consideration for the location of their own players. It would be very easy to say, "*Never* kick the ball toward your own goal," but to what advantage? In some instances that could be the best decision, and in later years players often kick the ball toward their own goal.

A way to avoid saying *never* in the early years of teaching a certain drill is to emphasize that decision-making is the consequence of responding to other players' actions, and this will change over time. It is important that your young players are allowed to make mistakes early and often, since this is how they learn the complexities of the game. As a result, they will sooner be able to play without the "coach crutch" of constant direction from the sideline.

The kids know the objective is to get the ball in the opponent's goal, so use the positive statement of "Move the ball toward the other goal." This is sufficient for most kids, but if you have a young player who can dribble well, he may decide to dribble toward his own goal to avoid players before turning toward the opponent's goal. This will be a great skill in later years, so you do not want to constrain this skilled player. And you do not want to coach in the negatives. So say what you want them to do, as much as possible, and try to avoid saying what you do not want them to do.

Share. Most children have been taught that they should share, so be careful when using this word on the soccer field. Much of soccer is about teamwork and cooperation, but early on the kids seem to polarize into two groups: those who never share the ball (ball hogs) and those who kick the ball away immediately (gift givers). Learning soccer includes learning to be the person between these two extremes: to know when to pass and when to keep the ball. The decision should be based upon what is best for the team over the long term. The parents and friends of the ball hog have probably told the player that if he keeps the ball and scores every time, then his will win. However, this will prevent the other players on the team from getting much practice and they will not get any better.

You must teach your players to share the ball and share the contribution to the team's success. When a player has the ball and the other team pressures him, the two primary options are to pass or dribble. When coaching the younger ages, it is important to teach the ball hog to pass and teach the gift giver to dribble, so they both increase their confidence in each other and the abilities of the team as a whole. As they advance in age and skill, the decision to share or not will be based largely on how the other team responds to each player, and they may have to change their strategy during the course of a game. For example, as the other team starts to overplay the pass, the gift giver may have to dribble the ball more.

You must introduce situations in practice where your players must exercise these decisions. For instance, most players know that they should pass if double-teamed; however, you must encourage the ball hog and gift giver to act in slightly different ways given the same situation in order to modify the behavior of the two extremes of ball possession. The gift giver will, hopefully, dribble the ball just a little bit longer and the ball hog will, similarly, pass the ball a bit more often.

With young players, it's difficult to teach the concepts of sharing with teammates and not sharing with the other team. Focusing on outcomes versus specific actions helps. Highlight helping the team to improve and succeed, rather than just to win.

Always. Always is the opposite of *never*, and while it is a positive, it can be equally confusing for kids. It is great to give kids clear direction, such as, "You are *always* correct to clear the ball away from the front of our goal." However, in certain situations using *always* can have the same negative effects as using *never*. For example, saying "always get the ball down the field as quickly as possible" may encourage your players to advance the ball when they should be backpassing or crossing the ball. As a result, using *never* and *always* may set you up for having to reteach skills. Your job is to help your players understand game situations and how to respond to them. Using *always* or *never* may make it easier to teach some soccer lessons, but you probably will have to have a meeting with your players the following year when they are better and more mature in their understanding and explain that what you meant by *always* is actually *usually but....*

For example, fullback play in the middle years is uniquely challenging, since it requires great decision-making. We suggest elsewhere in this book that you use an attacking fullback and another fullback, one in front of the other, rather than the typical side-by-side fullback arrangement. This permits the attacking fullback to be the one to first encounter the ball coming into his half of the field. We teach that the attacking fullback should be moving forward and that the fullback behind him should also be moving forward. This provides for a very aggressive, effective defense for the middle years.

However, this approach is not effective for the tween years, since as the opposition learns to pass and spread out, this always moving forward column of defenders is not as effective as defensively minded side-by-side fullbacks. As a result, you may have to reteach your fullbacks about how they play defense. Teaching this will take more time later or more time at the beginning; you must decide when your players are ready for the next step in complexity.

There is a tradeoff that you must decide upon. It is easier to teach simple techniques and use fairly decisive wording, such as, "Do not pass the ball in front of your goal," to peewee or middle year players. However, as the skill of your team progresses, you might find that you need to alter or re-teach a previous technique to account for the increased speed and strength of the team. At the same time, you probably do not want to explain every technique, drill, or process that might be adjusted later.

The key is to understand that when you use *never* and *always*, likely you will have to explain later that you really meant *usually*. This reteaching process is a great time to highlight to your players when you believe they are ready to move to the next level of soccer competency.

Should vs. *Can*. *You should* sounds like a command. It also sounds judgmental. *You can* is more inspirational. It sounds like you are reasoning with your players and getting them to think about their situation on the field. You are telling them they have options that they can use. You are empowering them. The key to good youth soccer hinges on this issue: the players need to make decisions and not just follow orders from their coach.

Sandwich, anyone?

Use the sandwich method when critiquing your players. Start off with a positive comment, follow with your teaching point, then close out with a positive comment. For example, if a young player is not getting into the correct position for transitioning the ball down the field, your interaction with that player might go like this: "Grace, I love the way that you are hustling out there and helping out your teammates. However, as a midfielder you need to keep away from the fullback so that you can help move the ball downfield. If you are right next to her, then you cannot really help her at all. Now go out there and keep up the good energy level!"

Team sport

Soccer is, at its best, a team sport. Players should take seriously their commitment to their team. This is an important life lesson. A team sport provides vital social interactions that will serve children for their entire lives. With the right mentality, kids can reap huge benefits from making this commitment. Putting the group's needs above his own is a tough concept for a child, but when he gets it, he becomes a better person. Depending on and trusting one's teammate to be in the right place at the right time is a complex, mature concept that is highly applicable to life off of the soccer field.

Pyramid of Soccer Power

We have hinted at the pyramid of power for soccer. First and foremost, thinking is foundation for the rest of the skills your players must learn. Thinking starts with how to learn the soccer positions and the simple rules of soccer. It also extends all the way to making split-second decisions on the field when two defenders are running right at a player.

Stamina, ballhandling skills, and teamwork are keys of the learning experience, all of which create an excellent soccer team and soccer experience. The purpose of these keys is to get everyone on the team in the right place: positioning. If a player is not in the right place, it does not matter if he can kick a soccer ball thirty yards with reverse spin with his left foot.

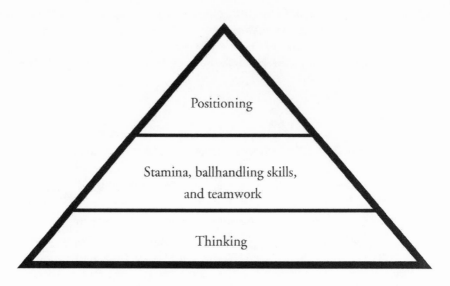

The pyramid of soccer power reinforces the importance of positioning and thinking.

Positioning is the top of this pyramid of power because it is the common factor in all great field teams. This manifests itself in the ability to make and deny space. This is a common thread among basketball, football, lacrosse, and many other team field sports. Making space and denying space are both done the same way: by anticipating (where the ball and players will go) and hustling. While making space is usually done for offensive reasons, denying space is a euphemism for good defense.

Creating and denying space

In preparation for writing this book, we discussed the material with many sports and academic experts. One dialogue that we had with a colleague, Babak Nouri, was particularly noteworthy. Babak was a college football coach at the Division I–AA and Division II levels for ten years. He held several coaching positions, including defensive coordinator, defensive backs coach, and quarter-backs coach for teams that won three conference championships and played in national playoffs and bowl games.

A summary of our dialogue follows, emphasizing the commonality of the focus on positioning in soccer with the same concept for football and basketball.

The concept of most any team sport, be it football, basketball, soccer, baseball, or hockey, boils down to the matter of creating or denying space that can lead to success (scores and denying scores). The offense is always looking to create the space that will lead to advancement towards scoring, and the defense is always designed to execute in a way that denies or narrows the space available to the opposing offense.

It is also important to remember that this battle of space occurs at both the individual player and overall team levels. If individual players cannot succeed in their one-on-one battles, it often, in turn, harms the integrity of the overall play the team is trying to execute, thus impacting the chance of success. Even more so, the simple use of terminology by players and coaches in games reinforces this concept. Many offensive players say "I'm open" and many defensive players are told to "contain" or "deny" their counterpart. Again these are terms used to describe space and the role each side has been cast in.

An example of this dynamic is the choreography of a simple pass play in football. At the start of the play, on an individual level, a wide receiver will make certain foot movements, and even head fakes, in order to deceive a defender and begin the process of getting down the field. On the other side of the ball, the defender assigned to that receiver has been told to "cover" or "jam" the receiver for the sole purpose of impeding the player's progress downfield. His individual assignment is to deny space to his counterpart.

At the same time, the quarterback drops back to read the defense's scheme and make the right decision, assuming that his offensive line will provide protection. The protection is designed to give the quarterback the necessary space to see the entire field through the concept of a "pocket" and easily deliver the ball via "passing lanes" to receivers through "windows." The defense, in turn, has the option to do one of two things, predetermined to limit the success of this play. They may choose to blitz to create pressure and deny the quarterback the room and visibility to throw the pass accurately, if at all. Alternatively, the defense may decide to stay back in a zone defense and narrow down the windows in which a receiver can catch the ball, thus reducing the chance of the play's success.

This concept is not unique to football. In basketball, teams will set up in a zone defense simply to deny the offense the quickest path to the basket or deny the shots that are much closer to the basket. Other defenses will "trap" the ball handler, pinning him between two defenders and a boundary on the court. The net result is that the offensive team's progress to the basket, either through dribbling or through a pass, is significantly impeded. Similarly, many offenses will run a "pick," where the team on offense will send a player at a defender guarding the player for the sole purpose of separating him from the ball handler. This, in turn, creates a pocket of space in which the ball handler can shoot the ball with a clear line of sight or make a pass to a teammate for an easy shot.

Babak's thoughts, while never mentioning soccer, are so relevant to this book and coaching youth soccer. The universal concept of *creating and denying space* is an essential part of soccer, especially soccer as a thinking game.

What Is Next?

Now it is time to discuss season milestones. No, you do not get to start reading about soccer yet. We want to focus on activities that reinforce the probability of you being a successful coach. Your success is more dependent on things that you do off the field then what you do on the field. This axiom is analogous to what we suggest you say to your players: "What you do without the ball is more important than what you do with the ball." As you will see in the next chapter, many significant events and activities during the course of a season have little to do with soccer but have everything to do with creating a positive season that will lay the foundation for your soccer players loving the sport.

CHAPTER 3
Season Milestones

Managing and communicating with league officials, parents, and players off the field will amount to ten times more effort than what you do on the field. However, the success of your team on the field is hundred times more dependent on what you do off the field than on it.

As a coach, you perform in three main areas: home, practice, and games. All of the early activities of a soccer season are done at home, before you or the players even see a soccer ball. The preparation at home and on the practice field prepares your team for the critical milestones of games, the end-of-season party, and picking all-stars.

At Home

If you are coaching a house soccer team, you will not normally get to select the children on your team. House soccer is the entry level of soccer and based on the maxim that everyone, regardless of skill level, should have an equal opportunity to participate. Depending upon the rules of your club, it may purposely mix up the teams each year, or let your team stay the same except for dropouts. Some leagues will form the teams based upon what school the children go to in order to maximize the likelihood that the children will know each other. No matter what the rules are, it is important to make an early positive contact with the parents of the children.

Once you get the roster from your division coordinator or equivalent, you should call each parent. Prepare a list of items to talk, including, but not limited to, the following:

• verify their e-mail address
• verify their home and cell phone numbers

• communicate your two or three primary goals for the season
• suggest probable practice times
• communicate your expectations for the parents
• ask for their help (such as team parent or assistant coach)
• make sure they have your contact information

The overall message you should communicate are that your team will have fun, learn soccer, and grow as a team. Emphasize the team over individual skills. Do not forget to tell both your players and their parents early and often that soccer is a thinking game.

One of the critical expectations to make clear to your players and their parents is that you will focus on improving team and individual skills over winning games. If you focus on having a winning season, then you are setting yourself up for potential failure. No one can guarantee a winning season. However, you can discuss that with hard work and regular practice attendance, you can expect the team to continually improve. You and your team *do* have control over whether or not they improve.

Handouts are critical to communication

Prepare a roster with all of the players' and parents' names, e-mails, and phone numbers. Include the practice fields and practice times on this sheet, so there is no doubt about practice obligations for the season. Once you get the information from your host club or league, you should also put the game schedule on the sheet. You will update this sheet throughout the year. You need to train your parents to read and post this sheet in the house. You do not want to hear, "I forgot we had practice on Thursdays."

Encourage carpooling. We have found that children who carpool make it to practices more reliably because they depend on each other. For the peewee and middle years, it is customary for parents to take turns bringing oranges or grapes for a halftime snack and a healthy treat after the game. Include these assignments on the team sheet as well.

The roster must include cell phone numbers for each parent, since that is what you need when you are driving to practice and you need to contact parents. The need for immediate communications may occur when there is lightning or a burst of rain, or one of the parents is lost getting to a new field. One year, our team parent made an index card-sized sheet that we could slip into a wallet or purse with team players' names and phone numbers so that all parents had all of the contact information with them when they got stuck in a traffic jam on the way to a game or practice or needed some last-minute assistance.

Lead by example. Since you say that soccer is a thinking game, you had better do some thinking yourself. Prepare handouts for use during the year that show positions and plays, for instance. Many of the diagrams included in this book are ones that we have used for our teams over the years. Think through what you want to get done for the season and document three clear goals that are challenging, measurable, and achievable. Do not say, "We want to win half of our games." As stated, you do not have control over winning or losing. You can, however, improve each game by having fullbacks transition the ball to midfielders on the outside from the goal every time, or having forwards stay in position when attacking, for example.

In the appendix of this book we have included several handouts that illustrate the type of written communication you can use throughout the course of the year.

Have a Plan

You should select at least three skills or team objectives each season for your team to master by your team. Use these core goals as a means to select drills, manage games, and reinforce vocabulary and motivational competitions. These objectives need to be challenging, measurable, and achievable.

Below is a sample matrix of objectives for the seven years that encompass youth soccer:

Category	Season	Season Objectives
Peewee	U6	• Watch the ball. • Everyone touches the ball at least three times each half. • "Go to the line" (explained in chapter 5).
	U7	• Watch the ball. • Everyone takes at least one shot during each half. • Everyone makes a pass to a teammate.
Middle Years	U8	• Dribble with both feet. • Pass to the open spaces. • Clear the ball from in front of our goal.
	U9	• Move to an open space when you do not have the ball. • Perform crossing passes from sideline to sideline. • Attack the ball.
	U10	• Use headers to control the ball. • Take quick shots on goal (do not dribble inside the opponent's 18 yard line). • Play strong defense inside our 18 yard line.
Tweens	U11	• Soft trap air balls with your thighs and feet. • Back pass three times a game (when appropriate) to an open player. • Mark up inside your 18 yard line ("hip on hip").
	U12	• Take shots from volleys (ball in the air, not on the ground). • The team should possess the ball 75 percent of the game. • Transition all goal kicks safely into the opponent's end of the field.

These objectives are listed in a sequence that you can alter depending upon the competency of your team. These are neither comprehensive (you can add some of your own) nor in a mandatory order, but merely some suggestions to guide results-driven coaching techniques.

Sometimes your team may not master a selected skill, so you will have to carry one goal over from a previous season. It is important to constantly focus on objectives you have control over, such as mastery of skills, and not winning or losing.

Your practices must simulate game situations so the players get comfortable with decision making and the stress of games. This will ease the transition when the games become more intense, both physically and mentally. Let your parents and their children know exactly what will be expected of them in this regard.

Youth are impressionable. They will copy what they see, both good and bad. You should be a role model. Many youth coaches are not that good at soccer, but that is okay. You should go out there and try to juggle the ball just like your players. The fact that some players are better than you is not a problem. They will see you trying over and over to get it right, so when they do not get a skill right away, they will remember that you were persistent when you could not quite "get it" and they will not get discouraged.

In this way, you will reinforce on the soccer field the life lesson that hard work is always a major factor in success.

Cognitive cones

You want to recruit many assistant coaches. They can help haul equipment to practice, show encouragement during practice, learn your coaching philosophy so they will be more agreeable on the sidelines, help coach all week long by reinforcing rules at home with their children, and even cover for you when something keeps you away from practice or even a game. However, one of the most important jobs of your assistant coaches is to serve as a "cognitive cone" during practice.

Cones can be distracting and confusing for youth soccer players and time-consuming for the coaches to arrange, so whenever you need a cone for the players to dribble around, use an assistant coach. This makes the coaches your cognitive cones. They think, they talk, they reason, and they interact with your players. At the peewee level, they will encourage the players as they run around them. In the middle years, they can provide some minor resistance by extending a leg or moving to make the drill slightly more challenging and realistic. For the tween years, we often use assistant coaches to fill in openings on scrimmages and play full speed with the players to provide an opportunity for coaching in game-like situations.

Team parent

The team parent is an important volunteer you need to recruit early. He or she has several responsibilities, such as ordering trophies at the end of the season, planning (with the coach) the end-of-season party, and obtaining gifts for coaches and assistant coaches. Usually the team parent will ask for some amount of money from the rest of the parents to cover these expenses. However, each team has its own personality, so your team may want to get medals or t-shirts to celebrate the season—or nothing at all. We believe there is way too much emphasis on prizes for just playing a game. When (or if) you move your team to travel (or elite) status, this ritual goes away. In travel soccer, you must *earn* your trophy by winning a tournament or a division.

At Practice

You need to plan out what you will do at your practices. We cover this thoroughly in chapter five, but the most important aspect of this preparation is the energy and enthusiasm that you must bring to the practice. If you want your players to give 100 percent, it is important that you do the same. Do not stand there with a clipboard and yell at the players to run. You should get up and run and kick the ball around with them.

First practice

Your first practice is your most important practice. You set the tempo for the season. You give and receive critical information. You get a feel for the personality of your team. So what do you talk about to break the ice at the first practice? Below are some general guidelines:

Peewee: Go over your players' names, ask their favorite food or color, talk to parents briefly (especially if you have not met them before), and, of course, let the players name the team by taking a vote. For ideas of names to suggest, go to some Web sites for other soccer leagues. This is an important and fun rite of passage. Enjoy this process; the kids will! Let everyone suggest their ideas, too, and then have them vote, by a show of hands, with their eyes closed. This makes it more exciting, and the children will vote more honestly if others are not watching.

Middle Years: Go over players' names, ask their favorite song or band, find out whether each player prefers offense or defense, and name the team.

Tweens: Go over players' names (there are usually few new players to soccer at this age, but be ready for that new player who needs to be brought into the already galvanized team), figure out what skills your players have, ask what is their favorite position, and name the team.

Game Day

Game day is what all the players and parents have been waiting for all week. E-mail or contact the entire team a day or two before the game to make sure everyone knows where and when to meet (everyone should arrive thirty minutes early), and remind the appropriate parent(s) to bring the snack.

You need to meet early for several reasons. First, this helps to ensure that even late arrivals will make it to the game before it starts. Second, the extra time gives the players enough time loosen up and relax. Third, it gives you time to talk to your team about the important objectives for the day's game.

Warming up before the game and getting the children ready to play always requires a balancing act. You want your players to get loose and think about what they need to do for the game, but you do not want to wear them out or get them nervous.

We identify drills in the upcoming sections, but we want to emphasize that the drills are only used before games to loosen up your players. Do not try to teach your players anything new during warm-ups. In fact, warm-ups are supposed to relieve stress and calm nerves. For this reason, simple kick arounds (have the players stand in pairs and kick the ball back and forth) are just fine.

For peewees, pick a favorite dribbling drill and have the kids do that for a few minutes. Do not let them get too tired. It is important that you emphasize the thinking part of the game at the outset, so ask the players a few simple questions regarding what you expect them to do. For example, you might ask, "What are the three things we need to do in the game today?" They might answer, "Watch the ball, find the line, and have fun!" ("Find the line" will be explained in the chapter five).

For the middle years, have the players warm up doing position-specific drills. Keep the concept of the game simple. Tell them that as long as each player does his job well, the team will do well. We have used the triangle drill for years because it is so versatile. The drill you select needs to reinforce what you want the players to do well. Shy away from shooting drills, since this comes so naturally and your focus should be on team aspects of the game. You do not need to worry so much about tiring out the players in this age group.

For the tween years, based the warm-ups on what you know the team needs to work on for this specific opponent, or how your team performs in the game normally. For example, if you know that you are playing a very physical team, you might warm up by having your team fight for the ball and/or maintain possession. If your team has started off slowly in recent games, you may want to focus on shooting drills. Older players have more stamina, so there is less chance of tiring your team during warm-ups, but you still have to be cautious. This is especially true if the weather is hot or you have few players to use as substitutes during the game.

Thinking

Have a chalk talk just before your players take the field. A chalk talk is when you use some visual aid to discuss positioning and spacing and set plays on the sideline. These mental exercises reinforce the role of all players in the flow of the game and make them think before they get on the field. This is a great time to remind your players that soccer is a thinking game and that what you do without the ball is more important than what you do with the ball. If they are in the right place (relative to the ball, the field, teammates, and the opponent), then they will only have to make a good play—not a great play—to help the team.

Talk about what your players should be doing in the game and show or draw a picture on paper or a dry erase surface. You can buy a magnetic clipboard with movable pieces from sports stores, such as Sports Authority and Modell's Sporting Goods, or Web sites, such as Kwik Goal (www.kwikgoal.com).

Using visualization before the game is important. It can help your players perform better. Ask them to close their eyes and visualize themselves the way they hope to approach the ball, control the ball, dribble the ball, pass the ball, move to an open space in order to receive a pass, move down the field staying in open space, transitioning to defense, tackling an opponent, or winning the ball back for your team. Pick some simple sequence each game that helps them rehearse in their own minds how they will perform the skills that they are learning. They will visualize the perfect form and the perfect outcome, which will help them perform better.

Sportsmanship

You must talk to the parents before the first game to reinforce that yelling at the players or referees is unacceptable. Razzing the referees provides a bad role model for the players and alienates them from your team. Parents should make only positive comments about their own team, to their own team. Never make comments about the other team. It is your responsibility to show the team how to exercise good judgment and sportsmanship.

Additionally, parents should not coach their child or any of your players. If a parent starts to provide tips about shooting, passing, positioning, or anything else, then offer for them to be an assistant coach. They can learn the system for the team, or return to cheers of "Good job!" and "Great hustle!"

Parents who offer tips can be counterproductive, since they may confuse the players if their advice contradicts what you've taught.

You also need to let the players know what you expect from them in terms of sportsmanship. This includes congratulating the opponent after the game, which often amounts to lining up the two teams (with the goalkeepers at the front of the line and coaches at the end), and then walking past each other shaking hands and saying "Good game." Sometimes it is as elaborate as the other team forming a human tunnel and having the other team run through it.

The rituals of youth soccer are as much fun and as important as the game itself. We have observed that girls usually have more of these rituals from cheers to face paint, than do boys.

The team in the dark jerseys is preparing a "tunnel" for the other team (after a hard-fought match), which the opposing team runs through while the "tunnel" team chants the other team's name.

In addition to congratulating the other team, you should make it a habit for your players to thank the referees. This often surprises the referees and the other team, but it reinforces the sportsmanship message. Over the course of the season, the referees will remember your team. Gratitude is especially important for youth soccer games, since the referees are typically teenagers or college students who need this positive reinforcement.

Team cheer

You may want a team cheer, but make sure that it reinforces what you want to achieve for the team. It is better to be boring and a good role model than fun and lose an opportunity to teach. One simple cheer that we used for years was "One, two, three, teamwork." The players and coaches all put their hands into the middle of a huddle of people, then at "teamwork" raise their hands up into the air. The following year, we wanted the players to focus on mental and physical toughness, so we changed the team cheer to "One, two, three, be tough!"

Below are a couple of favorite cheers that you might try on your team. You can do them in unison. Kids also enjoy doing them in volleys, where half the team does one phrase and the other half of the team does the next phrase, until you get to the final line, which they all yell together. (The cheers are alternately in roman and italic type to represent how your team might do the cheer in volleys.)

"Everywhere we go …"
Everywhere we go, *people want to know …*
Who we are, *so we tell them …*
We are the [team name]; *mighty, mighty [team name].*
The rough, tough [team name]; *the ball-kicking [team name].*
Go [team name]!

The following is a favorite of Devin from our CYA BLAST girl's team:

Barbie Cheer
We don't wear mini skirts, *we just wear our soccer shirts.*
We don't drink no lemonade, *we just drink our Gatorade.*
We don't play with Barbie dolls, *we just play with soccer balls.*
Go [team name]!

Girls seem to enjoy doing elaborate cheers more than boys do. However, selecting a basic cheer that reinforces the important theme for the season or for the game is useful for either gender.

Team captains

Before each game, the referees will ask for captains to have a coin toss. Alternate who will be the team captains. Everyone should get a chance during the course of the season. The kids really love to be the one at the center of the field when the referee flips the coin.

The players who serve as captains will come back and tell the team which goal your team will be defending and which team will kick off. Make sure that no matter what situation occurs, you congratulate the captains for a job well done: "Excellent! We want the wind to our back first. Good job, guys/ladies!"

Lineups and substitutions

For the peewee and the middle years, provide the starting lineup to your assistant coaches in advance so they know what to expect. Remember, though, that the head coach is the one who moves players in and out of the game. Before the game starts, tell the players who will be in the game first and who will be substituting for which teammates.

Try to avoid using words such as *starters* or the *first team*. The stigma of *not starting* demoralizes some children. Most leagues require some minimum playing time for players on your team until you transition to travel or elite status. Therefore, it is often a good idea to rotate who begins the match.

While you should always look to have the best combination of players on the field, it is good to have some continuity for young players when they are first learning how to play so they can increase their confidence.

When not playing, your players can drink a little water or give a quick hello to parents (if they are on their side of the field), but mainly they should watch the person playing their position on the field. They should be thinking all the time. Assistant coaches can spend time with the players not playing at the moment, noting what the other team is doing and how your players are performing.

Let your team know what you expect on the sideline as far as substitution. You should have two ironclad rules for your players: 1) stay nearby (on the bench, if you have one) so that when the coach needs to put you in, you are easy to find, and 2) do not ask, beg, or cajole the coach to put you in. Coaches love to have players who are ready to go in, but let them know that you do not want them to stand next to you and beg to go in. This is distracting. Let your players know this. It will help you a lot in the future.

For the tween years, you probably will not be able to plan out the substitutions as well. Put the first wave on the field and tell your team to be ready. You will substitute less often and more in response to how your players match up with the other team, rather than anything else. At this age, however, it is still critical to get everybody in every game.

In most house soccer leagues, everyone is required to play at least half of a game. For travel teams at this age, everyone should play some in every game.

Ideally, the fourteen to eighteen players on your team would be fairly inter-changeable, so that you would not have a drastic drop-off in your team's per-formance when substitutions occur.

There are two schools of thought about substitutions: waves or one-by-one. For the younger players, it is best to substitute in waves, or multiple players at a time. This enables you to easily manage the playing time and builds teamwork among a group of players. We call these subsets of the team squads.

As the players get older and the games get more competitive, you likely will need to make individual substitutions for a variety of reasons. First, your play-ers will start to get stronger and more conditioned, so they will be able to play at a high level for a longer period of time. Second, as the game goes from 5v5, then to 8v8, and then finally to 11v11, the amount of running each player will have to do will vary greatly from position to position, and the level of the con-ditioning may vary a lot between players. [Note: 5v5 means that each team has five players on the field at one time. Any configuration below the full 11v11 is considered playing a *short-sided* game.] Third, many coaches and trainers believe that it takes five to ten minutes for a player to really get acclimated to the game sufficiently to play near their potential. As a result, with older players you substitute less often and in smaller quantities (one or two at the most).

Try hard not to make substitutions after a mistake, no matter what the age of the players you are coaching. Try to substitute after an accomplishment (goal, great pass, good defensive stop, etc.) rather than a goal by the other team or a poor defensive sequence. You must help your team build confidence by show-ing confidence in them and maintaining the discipline and energy level during the match. When you do sub out some of your players, explain why they are being replaced, such as, "Take a little break and get your energy back."

You may need to modify this rule if you are working on a specific issue with a certain player and you want to discuss the issue right after a related incident occurs. For example, once we coached a good forward who kept trying to get the ball into scoring position all by herself. We had been working on her pass-ing the ball and then moving to open space downfield to receive the ball back via a wall pass. There was a great opportunity to do exactly this, but she passed it up, dribbled the ball down the field, and lost it to the other team. I took her out and asked her if she saw the opportunity. Indeed, she had seen the poten-tial for a pass. I then asked her whether or not there was a reason that she did not pass it. She said that she was afraid that she could not cross it accurately enough. Her incorrect decision was not due to the fact that she did not think, but rather based on her knowledge and perception of the situation.

We all thought that she was being a ball hog, but she had determined that she was better at dribbling than passing. The next few practices we worked on her confidence with passing. (Remember the general rule that boys lack focus and girls lack confidence). Since then this player has been one of the best forwards we have seen. The immediate discussion in the game gave us insight that was not obvious by what we saw.

Your goal as coach is to make thinking players. It is important to not assume that a player is doing something wrong if he does not do what you think he should have done. For example, after a questionable play, you should ask your player why he did what he did. If you think he should have passed the ball instead of taking a shot, you need to ask the player why he shot the ball. If the player does not know, then you need to work on decision making more.

If, however, the player said that he felt that the defense was anticipating the pass and the goalkeeper was not paying attention, then you have to concede to his better assessment of the situation. You can applaud the fact that the player thought out the play so well even if you disagree with his assessment of the situation. Over time, if the player is really thinking out his plays, then his ability to assess the intermediate visual cues (such as the "goalkeeper is not paying attention") will improve.

Coaching

Coaches should give clear directions from the sidelines, but keep your commands short. Resist telling players everything to do, such as, "Move to the right," "Get the ball," or "Pass to Emily." Preferably, you should *coach on the bench*, not *from the bench*. When the players get to the sidelines, talk to them there. Speak to your players plainly and calmly, but with energy and enthusiasm. Kneel down and get down on their level. Do not stand over your players and scream.

Coach D (Darren McKnight) is talking to part of his team during warm-ups, giving them a chance to hydrate, and discussing the few key points that are important for the game that day. Hannah, Emily, Alli, Jessie, Devin, and Grace are all listening. Notice that this is only half of the team. It is often better to have half of the team warm up while you go over specific points for the day with the other half, and then switch groups. This is an especially useful technique during hot summer tournaments.

Most comments from the coaches should be positive. Make constructive inputs loudly and make corrections quietly. Ridicule and sarcasm are not effective communication mechanisms on the soccer field or in life. Cheer for good passes, hustle, and good defensive plays more than for goals. This is true for coaches, parents, and players. It is also important that teammates use only positive words for each other.

Interactions with referees

Teach your players to respect referees. Refereeing soccer is a difficult and usually thankless job. You should emphasize that referees keep the game under control, and they do not prefer one team over another. They want the best team to win as much as you and your team do.

The coaches should never argue with the referees. If you have a problem with a referee, discuss the issue(s) at halftime in the presence of the other coach or after the game. Do not try to intimidate a referee into making calls your way.

This will always backfire; the referee will not see it your way because you are harassing him.

Worse yet, if your players hear you complaining about or to the referees, they will think they have the right to do the same thing. This will create two problems. First, the players may copy you and start arguing with the referees, which will quickly get them a warning (which will be embarrassing) or a penalty (which could really hurt the team). Second, your players will start thinking and talking about the calls that you are complaining about. This will take their mind and energy away from the game. The bottom line is, arguing with or complaining about the referee is always detrimental to your team.

After the game

After the game, make sure you have snacks for the peewees and middle years. This is a time to recover some of the fluids they expended during the game, but it is also a time to socialize and eat with the children and parents. This is a good time for your players to get more comfortable with each other and with you.

We learned early on to have healthy snacks after the game. Rather than donuts or cookies, the team parent can bring 100 percent juice drinks and pretzels or cheese crackers. You do not want to put the kids' blood sugar levels on a rollercoaster by following an energy-depleting game with sugar (candy and a soft drink). They will feel good for about thirty minutes and then come crashing down about the time they get home. The parents will wonder why their child is so cranky after a soccer game. They might think that their child loves soccer and hates to leave the field, when actually you have just wreaked havoc with their brains by coursing sucrose through their system!

Providing a healthy snack reinforces that good eating habits, like exercise, is lifelong.

Once the players get their snacks, make individual comments to every player before they leave. Be positive and as precise as possible. For example, instead of saying, "Great game, Mary," you should say, "I loved the way you cleared the ball to the halfbacks up the sideline rather than just kicking it out of bounds." You should be positive, but do not be afraid of slipping in some items that you will work on in practice. For example, "Jimmy, those were two awesome goals. I liked the way you shot the ball away from the goalkeeper. You had several other shots that were great attempts, but we will work next week in practice on passing the ball, rather than shooting, when a teammate is in a better position to score. You are getting better every week!"

Games should not be seen as culminations of practices, but rather as intermediate steps that allow the players to see some different talents, approaches, and strategies. It is imperative that you have a ritual before, during, and after the game to provide some continuity and comfort for the players. We will discuss more of the specific activities later, but all should focus on reinforcing confidence and making the experience fun. At the same time, you should try to minimize the chance for injury and maximize their ability to play well.

Encourage your players to *do their best*, not necessarily *be the best*. It is nice to be the best, but there is always some team that can beat you. However, no one can ever take away the satisfaction of your players playing better than the week before. We love the attitude of swimming in this aspect. The concept of having a *personal best* is the priority for swimmers. For all of the years of watching my daughters swim, I never heard anybody push them to win. I never heard anybody ask, "Did you win?" but rather, "Was it a personal best?" It is important to develop the same feeling among your players during the course of the soccer season.

During the season

As the season progresses, use quizzes to reinforce important points. This is more important with younger players, since older players have the skills. Advanced skills require more instinct and timing. You can also use motivational mechanisms in the middle of the season to keep the kids' interest high. For example, you might agree that every crossing pass that goes more than fifteen yards counts as five points, and once the team has one hundred points, you will bring an extra treat for the team. One year, I had the BLAST Frosty Frenzy, where the team got ten points for every header performed and five points for trapping the ball in the air. Once they had received two hundred points, I bought them all a small milkshake.

This is also the time to change some of the warm-up drills. For example, if you have seen opponents taking the ball from your players often when they are dribbling, then you might practice the stiff leg drill (see chapter five) to get them warmed up and thinking about how to maintain control when the other team attempts a tackle. (A *tackle* is an attempt to steal the ball and/or stop the forward movement of an opponent that has the ball.)

Changing players' positions

As the season progresses, think about how much you move your players around into different positions. For peewees, it is imperative that you move the players all over the field. Do not think that a player should always be on offense or always on defense.

For the middle years, start figuring out where the natural skills of your players are best applied, but do not be afraid to experiment. When moving the players around, let them know in advance. Mention it to them in practice, well before game day, and have them practice that position some.

For the tween years, you will need to get the parents involved. Let them know why you are trying their child at a different position, but do not let them push you toward a position that is not best for the child or for the team. Some parents have a tendency to focus too much on their child being the big scorer. This is why it is important to make it clear early that a goal is always the result of the effort of many players (usually all of those on the field), not just the last person who touches the ball before it goes into the goal.

End-of-Season Party

Usually after the last game, the team will have an end-of-season party. This party is even more important than the last game. Most leagues encourage the purchase of trophies for each member of the team, but we think this sends the wrong message to the young players. The sport is exciting, the exercise is refreshing, the social aspects are fun, but why a trophy? However, if parents insist on rewarding the players with a trophy, do not try to stop them. You will just get grief for it. You can do many other things during the end-of-season party that are useful and reinforce positive life lessons.

We always provide a quiz at the party that is about soccer but may have some silly questions to make it more fun. A sample U8 quiz follows:

Soccer Quiz–Teach soccer and have fun!

1. What position(s) do you play? _____

2. Who won the World Cup this year? _____

3. What other position are you most likely to be <u>passing to</u> when we are transitioning from defense to offense (the ball is going from our end of the field to our opponent's end of the field)? Explain. _____
_____
_____

4. What size soccer ball do we use? _____

5. When the other team pushes the ball down the field on our left side, our fullback will move toward that side of the field. Who will take up the weakside (in this case, the right side of the field) fullback?
_____
If the fullback has to go all the way to the left corner to pressure the other team, which has the ball, then who takes over the strongside (in this case, the left side) fullback?
_____

6. If the other team presses the ball down the middle of the field, the center midfielder has the primary responsibility to slow down or stop the other team. If the center midfielder is beaten (the other team gets past her), the fullback will attack the ball. Where will the center middie go?
a. Attack the person who has the ball along with the fullback.
b. Run to the sideline and ask the coach what to do.
c. Pretend to be hurt so that they ref stops the play.
d. Run straight to our goal in order to rotate back into the fullback's position.

If the attack comes straight up the middle (with the center middie and the fullback rotating as discussed in Question 6), I did not say what the outside midfielders do. What do you think would be the best thing for them to do? (Hint: this answer is not in the handout. Think!)
_____
_____
_____

The quiz itself is not really important; how you use it is critical. We hand out the quiz and say that every player can get the help of anybody at the party, including parents, siblings, friends, and other players. We also tell the children that we have a prize for the winner and hint that to get the prize the winner will have to use all of the skills learned during the season, especially teamwork. In this way, we try to get all of them to work together and submit only one quiz.

We usually start to see clumps of kids doing the quiz, and then they start to assemble into larger groups. We are really tough on the quizzes that come forward with only one name on it, and usually after five or six quizzes, with a mistake or two, we will get a perfect quiz. We then give out the prize to the winner, such as a number of identical packs of sugar-free gum, pencils, and little soccer balls. The number of items always equals the number of players on the team, so that the winning group immediately understands that they are to share with the entire team.

The end-of-season party is an important time to thank parents, assistant coaches, and siblings. The most important part of the party, besides having fun, is to reinforce the learning experience of the soccer season with some type of memento. We have used a variety of techniques over the years that have proven to be winners. The problem is that if you retain many of the players from season to season, you have to work hard to look different each season. As part of the end-of-season party, it is the coach's job to hand out the mementos (such as player cards, nickname certificates, personalized soccer gear, etc.) and say something to each of the kids. Handing the trophy to each child and saying his name is what most coaches do, but you should do more.

Try one of the following techniques to liven up the "awards ceremony":

Official team nickname. Come up with a positive nickname for each child. Start to talk about the child without giving his name and see if the other players can figure out who you are talking about. At the end of the introduction, announce the player's official nickname. For example, when our team was the Black Bats, I would decree the "Official Black Bat Nickname" for each child. The kids will talk about this nickname for many months, even up to the following season. Make sure the nicknames are positive and reinforce some good attribute the player has.

Here are some of the example nicknames that we have given out over the years:

Racie Gracie (since Grace was so quick).
The Enforcer (since Jessie was so tough).
The Rocket (since Alli was so fast).
The Natural (since Kaitlyn was excellent at every aspect of the game).
Jailbreak Jessie (because when she came dribbling down the field the whole team followed).
Ironman Dan (since Danielle played so tough).
Spider Woman (since Brianne seemed to be able to shoot out webs and pull in the ball and other players).
Alli Einstein (since Alli made so many smart plays).
The Spear (since Jen loved being at the point of attack).
Tower of Tenacity (since Hannah fought so hard).
Titan (since Jordan's punts were so far and high it was as if she was launching soccer balls into orbit, like the Titan launch vehicle).
Debutante Devin (since the season was a breakout season for Devin).

You can imagine how it gets difficult over several seasons with the same children to come up with new nicknames each year.

Certificate suitable for framing. We make a PowerPoint certificate with pictures of our team namesake (such as Black Bats or Tigers) and photos of the player that she can put up on her bulletin board. It makes me feel good to go over to one of my daughter's friend's house and see one of these certificates, tattered and torn, still hanging on the refrigerator or the her bulletin board.

Player cards. Take a photograph of each child and make a mockup of a player's card, like the ones you can buy of professional football players and baseball players. These are also available with many of the standard team photography services used by recreational leagues.

Personalized soccer gear. Many kid-friendly, reasonably priced soccer-related items are available for purchase. Go to any large sporting goods store that sells trophies and/or team uniforms. We have used or know of other teams that have used pencils, decals, necklaces, wristbands, SweetSpots (large rubber bands that go over cleats to hold in laces and show where the ball should strike the foot), t-shirts, and medals, for example.

Picking All-Stars

For the house soccer league, the requirement at the end of the season of picking all-stars can be emotional. The post-season all-star tournament provides an opportunity for some select players to extend their season and play on a temporary team for a week or two. Sometimes, the league provides guidance as to how you should select your all-stars, but usually you select the best players on your own.

Some coaches either pick their players at random or pick the best players who had not had the chance to go before. We disagree with both of these approaches. You should select the best players even if the same ones are selected every season. However, you should always ask all of the assistant coaches to vote on the all-stars and select the players with the most votes. This provides you with the cloak of consensus so the parents cannot complain (but they still might). Do not announce to the entire team which of your players were selected to be the all-stars until the players reach the tweens stage.

This is a life lesson. You will have good players, average players, and below-average players. Your job as coach is to meld them into a good team. The below-average player in peewees may hit a growth spurt and a personality change that makes him a good middle years teammate and an excellent tweens player. So, do not let whether or not a player is selected to be an all-star drive him away from playing soccer.

Dealing with Parents

Most disagreements and friction with parents stem from different expectations, so it is important to communicate early and often what your expectations for the team are. While many coaches believe that this means talking, it really is more about listening. There are all types of parents, but they usually fall into one of three camps: balanced, ambivalent, and psycho.

Balanced parents are the ones who see soccer for their young children as a game. To them, it is as much social as sport. They evolve as their children's ambition and interest in soccer changes. If their child ends up not liking soccer, they graciously listen to their child and let them try another activity. If their child is good and really enjoys soccer, they will be the first to volunteer to help with the team and support your efforts to coach soccer. You want balanced parents, but it is hard to tell what type of parents you have, at least for a few months, if not a season or two.

Ambivalent parents really do not care much about soccer. They signed up their kid for soccer because it was convenient and less expensive than a baby-sitter or because they could carpool with the neighbor kid (whose parents are probably balanced). Ambivalent parents do not cause problems, but they also rarely help. Ambivalent parents are fairly low maintenance, but they do not provide the kind of support structure you need as you take a team into the tween years and beyond.

Psycho parents are rare, but they are more numerous than you might expect. A psycho parent keeps score during peewee games, complains about the referees in the middle years, and provides you unsolicited advice about who should play during the tween years. They will be the first ones to come to you if their child is not playing enough. They will also be the first ones to leave a team that is not winning enough. You can best manage psycho parents by making them assistant coaches and helping them to understand the complexities of a coach's job. You can rein in psycho parents, but it is difficult. You must manage their expectations, put them to work as a volunteer, and be honest with them from the beginning.

The worst thing that a coach can do is to assume that their parents know the rules of the game or of the league. At the peewee level, most leagues do not keep score and, therefore, do not have champions. It is important to tell the parents and the kids this at the first meeting or practice.

The next big issue will be playing time for your players. In peewee and the middle years, I would print out a table that showed when I would substitute players at predetermined times so that by the end of the year every player had the same amount of playing time. I even took into consideration when a player missed a game due to sickness. Showing this to parents at the beginning of the season and using it every game eliminated this issue, whereas many of my coaching colleagues dealt with ongoing feuds about playing time. As mentioned, this usually is less of a problem in the tween years since substitutions and the level of play are so different.

The last big topic of discussion with parents is the position on the field that their children will play. In most cases, parents want to see their kids score goals. Again, for the peewee and middle years, I made a habit of rotating players through multiple positions. Many coaches put all players through all positions, but we do not recommend that. If you do not let your players get comfortable at a position before you move them to another position, then they might start to lose confidence in their soccer ability, the team may perform poorly because several players are confused at once, and your players' efforts may be tentative since they lack the confidence to perform.

I found that it was important, especially for girls, to fit a child's physical and emotional strengths to a position on the field and then play her there consistently (but not exclusively). Give all your players a chance to excel early in their soccer experience so that they maintain a level of excitement. Just as with the parents, talk to your players often about your decisions and why you make them. For instance, you may have a child who has great decision-making skills, but who is not very good at dribbling. This person in the middle years might make a great defender or fullback. Putting the player in that position permits her to make important plays for her team and highlights her strengths rather than their weaknesses.

What Is Next?

The next chapter, "Basics of Soccer," provides a summary of critical facts that a youth soccer coach needs to know. It covers both items that are important to know and those that are often misunderstood. This is not an exhaustive compendium of soccer information, but it is sufficient for coaching youth soccer.

CHAPTER 4
Basics of Soccer

Before continuing, it is instructive to define some terms for soccer related to the field of play, basic plays, and commonly misunderstood rules. If you have played soccer before, then proceed on to the next chapter.

Field of Play

Every soccer field is rectangular, with a halfway line and goals at opposite ends of the field. However, the size and area markings change drastically as kids progress through youth soccer.

The following list shows the progression of field size in youth soccer (Source: Virginia Youth Soccer Association). These may vary slightly from state to state and from country to country, but the general trend is clear. The field gets larger and the number of players on the field increases for the older age groups.
- Under 6: 3 v 3 (no goalkeeper); Field: 20 x 25 yards
- Under 7: 4 v 4 (no goalkeeper); Field: 23 x 40 yards
- Under 8: 4 v 4 (no goalkeeper); Field: 23 x 40 yards
- Under 9: 6 v 6 (including goalkeeper); Field: 40 x 60 yards
- Under 10: 6 v 6 (including goalkeeper); Field 40 x 60 yards
- Under 11: 8 v 8 (including goalkeeper); Field 50 x 90 yards
- Under 12: 8 v 8 (including goalkeeper); Field 50 x 90 yards
- Under 13: 11 v 11 (including goalkeeper); Field 60 x 100 yards
- Under 14: 11 v 11 (including goalkeeper); Field 60 x 100 yards
- High School Recreational: 11 v 11 (including goalkeeper); Field: 70 x 110 yards

Similarly, the ball size used by each age group changes over time:

- Up to Under 8 (U8): size 3
- Under 9 (U9) to Under 12 (U12): size 4
- Under 13 (13) and older: size 5

The peewee field markings vary drastically by state, county, and even league. However, once you get out of peewee, most of the major markings are used. The figure below depicts the soccer field with key features. The diagram is not to scale, since there is a reasonable amount of variation among the layout of these features as teams move through the age groups.

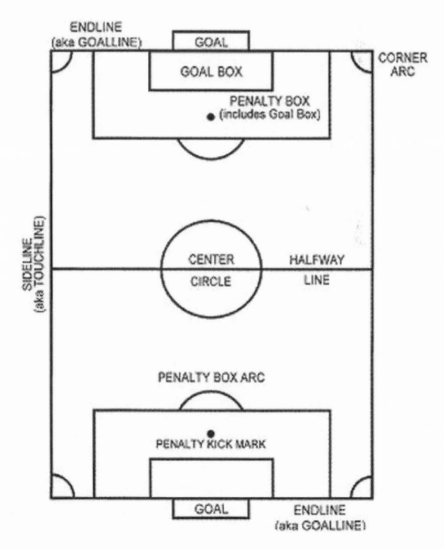

Thirds, not halves

While the soccer field is separated by the halfway line into halves, think of the field as being divided into thirds. Your third goes from your goal to just outside your 18 yard line. This is considered the defensive third; the urgency and precision required in this region are emphasized in this book. Suffice it to say for now that neither the ball nor the other team should be allowed to linger in this region. Emphasize to your team that this is not a good place for fancy moves. Instead, they should just clear the ball to a teammate.

The middle third goes from just outside your 18 yard line to just before your opponent's 18 yard line. This is the transition zone. In this area, each team fights for possession and tries to move the ball into a scoring position.

The last third is the offensive third. This area extends from just outside your opponent's 18 yard line to its goal. This is where your team must be aggressive and take advantage of possessions to create scoring opportunities. This is also the portion of the field where you should encourage the most risk, imagination, and creativity.

So in summary, take no risks in your third of the field, minimal risks in the middle third, and reasonable risks in your opponent's third.

Peewee field

The peewee field normally has two small, pop-up, hemispherical goals, one at each end of the field. Usually, a keep-out zone is painted in front of each goal, since there are no goalkeepers at this level.

Basic Plays

You need to know a few basic plays in order to start coaching. You will likely encounter these basic plays at least once in any game for the middle years or tweens.

Corner Kicks

A corner kick is awarded when the ball goes out of your opponent's end line (behind the goal that your team is shooting at) and is last touched by one of your opponents. One of your players will be able to set the ball at the corner arc on the side of the goal the ball left the field. He can then kick it toward the goal once the referee signals that it is okay to proceed.

There are no corner kicks in peewee soccer, but in the middle years and tween years, they become increasingly important. The primary objective when first executing a corner kick is for your team to at least maintain possession. You have two options when first performing corner kicks in the middle years:

1.   Kick the ball toward the goal box and hope for the best.
2.   Kick the ball to a teammate positioned near the 18 yard line, who can then pass it along to players closer to the goal.

Be patient. Corner kicks are not potent offensive weapons in the early years of youth soccer. They are merely another opportunity for getting the ball into play.

As the players get strong enough to get a corner kick to the goal box while it is still in the air, or if your players are skilled at passing, everything changes. When your players get to this point, you need some simple set plays for corner kicks. Your options depend upon who is taking the corner kicks. Always decide who is going to take a corner kick before it is time to take one.

We have taken three different approaches over the years. (The field positions will be discussed in detail in chapter five. However, for this chapter it is sufficient to know that halfbacks/forwards play toward your opponent's end of the field, fullbacks play close to your goal, and midfielders play in the middle of the field.)

In the first approach, the center midfielder takes the corner kick. However, this takes one offensive player out of the play. A second option is for the outside midfielder on the side of the corner kick to take the kick, but that would weaken the ability of your team to prevent your opponent from quickly transitioning. The third option we have tried is for the fullback to race up to take the corner kick. This leaves all of the offensive players in place but requires the fullback to hustle back into position, especially if the corner kick is poorly struck.

You should teach three common plays to your team first. Once you have mastered these corner kicks, then you can get one of the many books that explain dozens of corner kicks, or just experiment on your own. Remember, you have emphasized the need for your players to experiment and try new approaches; you should do the same thing. Do not be afraid to be creative and make up some of your own corner kick plays.

Corner kick one: basic press

In the basic press, line up your forwards (or halfbacks, your frontline of offense) just outside the goal box and have them run toward the goal just as the ball is being kicked toward the goal. If you are coaching a team in the middle years, you hope that the forward momentum of the players might knock the ball into the goal. However, as your players enter their tween years, you should start looking for your players to volley (kick the ball in while it is in the air) or head (use their head to direct the ball) the ball into the goal.

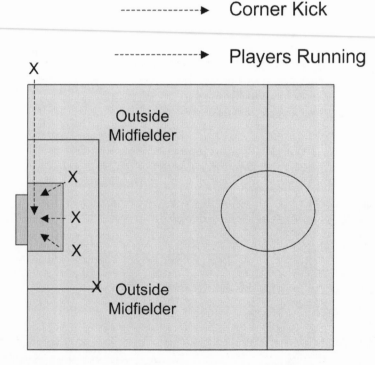

The basic press, shown in the figure above, is simple and sets up the next corner kick play, the counterflow.

Corner kick two: counterflow

For the counterflow kick, everyone lines up as they would for the basic press, except that about a second or two before the corner kick is executed, the weak-side forward (the forward on the side of the field where the ball is not located) runs through the goal box. This counterflow (the player runs *toward* the ball, which is opposite from what is expected) may move some of the defenders out of the goal box by using this forward as a decoy; it may confuse the goalkeeper; or it may put this moving forward in a position to control a poorly executed corner kick.

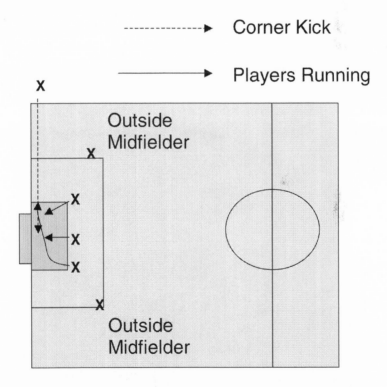

The counterflow corner kick play requires some practice to get the timing down between the kicker and the weakside forward.

The sequence of events in a counterflow corner kick is as follows:

1. Kicker sets up to strike the ball and raises one arm about one second before stepping toward the ball.
2. The weakside forward runs through the goal box, making it to the goalpost closest to the corner kick just as the ball gets there.
3. The weakside forward lets the ball go through if it is above his hips.
4. If the ball is on the ground, the weakside forward intercepts it and directs it to the strongside (the side of the field where the ball is located) outside midfielder, who either shoots it, lofts the ball into the front of the goal, or crosses it to the weakside outside midfielder.

Corner kick three: control and center

The first two corner kick plays are fairly effective only if the person performing the corner kick can reliably get the ball high in the air in front of the goal. Otherwise, you may have to use the control and center play. This play also may be effective if the other team is overplaying the first two types of corner kicks.

The strongside midfielder gets the ball directly from the corner kick and then either shoots or centers the ball to the weakside midfielder, who moves to the center of the field. This player is effective if the opposing team puts all of its players into its goal box.

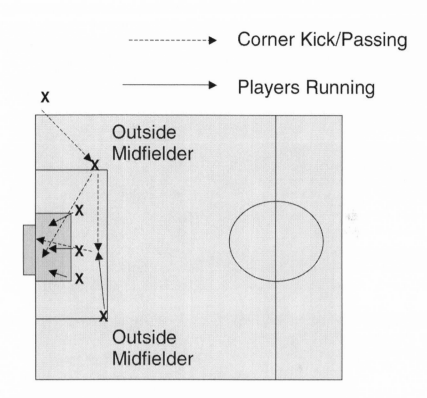

The control and center play provides an interesting alternative to the typical corner kick play.

Defending corner kicks

When defending corner kicks, remember what you are trying to do with your own corner kicks, since that is basically what your opponent will be trying to do to your team. The other team is trying to score a goal, so those players will be aggressively pressing the ball toward your goal.

The first way to thwart a corner kick is to prevent it from getting in front of the goal. Place the forward on the side of the corner kick midway between the corner kick arc and the goal, just a few feet from the end line. It is critical that this player does not let a ball get in toward the goal along the end line; if the ball makes it in front of the goal, it will not require much of a shot for your opponent to score. As your players get older and stronger, corner kicks will be struck

Soccer is a Thinking Game

in the air. Until then, you might keep the ball away from your goal by trying to block the initial corner kick.

The next line of defense is to remember that no one can score without the ball, so play the ball. Fill the space around your goal with players, evenly spaced, so that no matter where it goes you can get to it. This works great in the middle years, since the ball almost always will move faster than your opponent. You have just as good of a chance to get the ball as your opponent as long as your remain evenly spread out.

However, as your team approaches the tween years, the players' foot speed, quickness, and foot strike all improve to the point that the strategy must change a bit, away from playing the ball to playing your opposition's players. A well-timed, fast run on the goal with the corner kick is nearly impossible to stop without disrupting the movement of the player who is closing on the ball. Therefore, the rule for your players is to mark up against the opposing players and keep between them and your goal, so that they do not have a straight run or shot at your goal. Challenge your team to be the first to touch the ball during an opponent's corner kick. If your players are moving away from your goal, then your team, if quick, can usually thwart a corner kick. However, if you have a quick team running toward your own goal, it is fairly likely that one of your players will knock the ball into your goal. Minimize the chance for this deflating occurrence by emphasizing to your players that they should concentrate on moving away from their own goal during an opponent's corner kick.

Goal Kicks

Goal kicks are executed when an attacking team knocks the ball out of an opponent's end line. The ball is placed on the front edge of the goal box and then kicked downfield. While the goal kick is supposed to provide an advantage to the kicking team, no play in youth soccer has a greater potential to backfire.

The primary objective of any goal kick is to maintain possession of the ball and then get the ball downfield. In the middle years (there are no goal kicks in peewee leagues), few kids can actually kick the ball far enough to reliably put the ball into play, especially since the goal kick must get out of the 18 yard line before either team can play the ball. This is a real problem for the middle years.

The goal kick is a wonderful opportunity to reinforce the importance of sound decision making and reacting to what your opponent does. You will need to consider these three steps:

1. *Who kicks the ball?* In the middle years, a fullback routinely does the goal kick so that the goalkeeper can stay in the goal, in case the ball is not played reliably to a teammate. It is imperative that you have a fullback who can kick the ball relatively well and accurately. In the tween years, goalkeepers are more likely to execute the goal kicks. This leaves more players available to receive the goal kick and contribute to transitioning the ball downfield.

2. *Where are the players on the field?* The team performing the goal kick must spread out in order to both create space (by spreading out the opposing players) and to provide more options for the kicker.

3. *Where is the ball kicked?* Once the players are distributed about the field, the person performing the goal kick must decide where to kick the ball. Obviously, the options are partially dependent on where the players are, but also on how well someone can kick the ball. If your midfielders are taller than your opponents, then your fullback or goalkeeper might try to kick more in the air toward your midfielders, since it is likely that they would win the ball through a header. An advantage in foot speed might cause your team to simply kick the ball toward an outside open space and then just outrace your opponents to the ball.

For the middle years, there are two likely plays for the goal kick: sideline outlet or shoot-the-gap.

The sideline outlet is a short pass to an outside midfielder or fullback, who is placed directly toward the sideline rather than downfield. This play gets the ball out from in front of the goal but not down the field yet. From the sideline, a poor pass or turnover to the other team is not as potentially dangerous as it would be from in front of the goal. In addition, if your opponent is overplaying the center of the field, then your players can navigate around them by going to the outside first and then down the field.

The shoot-the-gap play is exactly what it sounds like. The person taking the goal kick looks for the largest gap in the defense and then kicks it hard through the gap. Knowing that this play can be effective directly affects how your team should defend against goal kicks: spread out and keep the ball in front of you.

For the tween years, there are more options for goal kicks, but also more risk if your players make the wrong decision or execute poorly. You can use the sideline outlet or the shoot-the-gap. However, the leg strength of tween players permits the kicker to select an opening downfield and kick the ball in the air over the first line of defenders. This capability is not normally available in the middle years, necessitating careful spacing of your players.

Defending goal kicks

Your opponents will have the same problem with everything that we warned you about in executing goal kicks. As a result, the best way to defend goal kicks is to exploit your opponent's weaknesses. Follow these three rules for defending goal kicks:

1. *Challenge them*. Have the strongside forward play just outside the 18 yard line, directly in front of the person doing the goal kick so that the kicker has to kick the ball around or over your player. Once you know that your opponent has either a strong or an accurate person doing the goal kicks, you probably should move the strongside forward back.
2. *Keep the ball in front of you*. It is usually better to let the ball get into play but have it stay in front of your offensive players, so have your players move back until they know that the ball will not go over their heads. However, they may need to be ready to attack the ball moving toward your opponent's goal.
3. *Spread out*. If your players are back far enough so that the ball stays in front of them, then they need to spread out in order to make it more difficult for the opponents to kick it past your offensive players. As we have stated, a primary objective on the field is to deny space when you do not have the ball and make space when you do have the ball.

Free Kicks

A free kick is awarded when another team is penalized for some infraction in the open field. The free kick will be either a direct kick or an indirect kick. In either case, the opposing team (the team not getting the kick) has to be at least ten yards from the player performing the free kick.

An indirect kick can be kicked in any direction, but it is usually kicked downfield toward the opponent's goal. However, it cannot go directly into the goal and count as a goal. Someone else on the field must touch it first. The other player to touch it can be from either team. A tricky play that many teams do is have one player run quickly by the ball and gently taps the top with his cleat, and then a second player comes in for the crushing blow toward the goal. You will know that the kick is indirect when the referee holds his arm above his head until the ball is touched by a second player.

An extremely difficult to play to handle is when someone takes an indirect kick directly at your goalkeeper and he instinctively tries to save it. If the ball goes through his arms or hands and then into the goal, it counts as a goal because the goalie touched it. If the goalie had just let it go into the goal, then it would not have counted. It is difficult to expect a young goalkeeper to be so disciplined as to know when to just let a ball go sailing into the net, but this is one thing you can teach older players. It is common to start to instruct your goalkeeper on these issues when the players move to full-sided games at the age of thirteen or fourteen.

A direct kick may be kicked directly into the goal. It is a live ball as soon as the kicker strikes it. If a player is penalized while inside his own penalty box, then the direct kick becomes a penalty kick. For a penalty kick, the ball is placed in the penalty box arc and all of the players from both teams are moved out of the way except for the kicker and the goalie. For a normal direct kick, all of the players stay on the field and jockey for position, similar to a corner kick.

After a free kick has been stuck, play continues normally. This is important to note because often a team will let down if a direct kick is blocked; however, if the ball is rolling around, it is still a live ball and can be kicked in for a score.

Commonly Misunderstood Rules

Normally, the league in which you coach will provide rules for you to follow. However, we will start you with several general regulations to provide a solid framework for understanding your league-specific rules. Note that most of the following rules and insights apply only to the middle years and tweens, not to peewee soccer.

Handling, not handball

There is no infraction called "handball." It is called "handling" when a player purposely touches the ball with his arm/hand *and* moves the ball into a favorable position to his team. This is the most often misunderstood call mainly because it requires two subjective decisions by the referee at once.

Out of bounds

The ball is considered out of bounds only after the entire ball is beyond the outside edge of a field line. A similar rule applies for when a goal is scored: the ball must completely cross the end line in the goal. Many parents and children mistakenly assume that a goal has been scored when the ball is more than halfway across the line or if it simply touches the line.

In addition, a player may be out of bounds when he plays a ball that is in bounds. Many youth players and their parents get confused about this. Out of bounds it is about where *the ball* is, not where the player is. This confusion may because American football has different rules.

Physical play

Roughness is part of soccer. If your children do not want to be touched, you may want to direct them toward swimming, track, or dance. A player may make body contact with another as long as he is playing the ball and not just knocking into the other player in order to get access to the ball.

A starting youth coach should reinforce three general rules:

1. *Play the ball.* Players need to get their hips over the ball. If it looks to the referee as if your player is using his body to prevent another player from getting to a ball he does not possess, your player will be called for a foul. However, if your player's primary focus is to attack or control the ball and the contact with the opponent is incidental to this primary intent, your player probably will not be called for a foul.

2. *Do not extend your arm.* Once a player's arm is extended to another player, the referee is much more likely to call a foul. However, if you can teach your players to hold their elbows close to their side, then they

can make solid contact with their shoulders and hips without getting called for a foul.

Both girls battling for the ball above are doing a good job of keeping their arms in. However, Lacy (in the dark jersey) will win this ball because she got better position by getting her hips over the ball.

Grace (in dark jersey) is keeping her arms in and her hips over the ball while the girl in the light jersey has extended her arm to try to prevent Grace from controlling the ball. The referee blew the whistle a few moments later and called the player in the white jersey for a foul.

3. *Do not make contact with the back of an opponent.* If the opponent whom your player is attacking cannot see him, then your player will probably be called for a foul. Subtle pressure on an opponent's back is acceptable as long as your player is trying to get to the ball.

Offside

Two events must occur before the referee calls offside. Before we examine those two events, however, let's think about why there is offside. Offside is called to prevent a player from just kicking the ball down the field to a teammate standing nearby an opponent's goal hoping for an easy shot. The intent of offside is to require a team to bring the ball down the field and not just play kickball.

So the first condition in an offside call is for a player to be in an offside position at the *moment* the ball is played (or touched) by a teammate. To be in an offside position, a player must be on the opponent's half of the field. In addition, the player also must be closer to the opponent's goal line than both the ball *and* the last defender (not the goalkeeper).

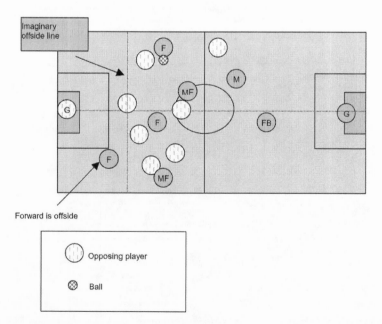

Forward is offside

Offside is a difficult concept for the youth soccer player since it requires watching several players at once.

The second condition is that the offside player must be involved in active play by gaining an advantage from being offside or interfering with an opponent. In other words, if a player is in an offside position but never touches the ball, on onside player can still continue the play.

It is important to remember that a player can never be offside when on his half of the field. This is useful if you can transition the ball quickly against an overly aggressive offensive team. For example, if your opponents are all in your half of the field, one of your forwards can head for their goal. As long as the ball crosses the halfway line before they return to their half of the field, your player is not offside.

For more detailed soccer rules, you can access current rules for your league from its Web site. You also can find a good set of rules at SoccerHelp.com (www. soccerhelp.com).

Substitutions

Making substitutions in games is often stressful for rookie coaches. In pee-wee soccer, substitutions may be done at a variety of points, but the leagues differ greatly. Usually, they can be done at the end of periods or after a score.

For the middle and tween years, you can normally make substitutions at five times in a game:

- On your own goal kick (though some leagues will let both teams substitute on any goal kick)
- On your own throw-in
- After a score by either team
- At the beginning of a half
- When the other team removes a player due to injury

How you make substitutions is important. You can take two fairly different techniques: waves or singles/pairs.

Substituting in waves

When you substitute in waves, you let the team that starts the game stay in the game for five to ten minutes (depending upon their stamina) and then substitute in everyone you can. This may mean that for a 6v6 game, you would replace everyone except for the goalkeeper at once. The benefit of this approach is that your waves can create a bit of chemistry among these groups. One year, I asked the girls to give their squads their own name and built up a bit of competition about which squad scored the most goals and held their opponents to the fewest.

Unfortunately, this may not allow some players to get into the flow of the game, which might discourage some players or hold some back. This is not a significant issue in the early years because you really cannot tell who needs the longer time on the field versus who needs the rest. However, playing time is often one of the primary reasons parents and children want to move to travel or elite soccer teams. On those teams, coaches need not play all the kids the same amount of time, so waves of substitutions are not necessary and usually not wise.

Substituting in singles/pairs

Some coaches believe that it takes about five to ten minutes for players to become comfortable out on the field, so if you substitute everyone at once then your team's effectiveness will drop abruptly. Even though everybody is fresh, they will not be in the flow of the game. In this case the singles/pairs substitution would be a better option. In this scenario, you substitute players one or two at a time, depending upon who needs the rest or how the other team is doing relative to your team.

Another benefit to the singles/pairs substitutions is that you can pair up a stronger player with a weaker player on the field. This provides stability for the team and a means for players to learn from each other. For example, a weaker fullback will be more aggressive knowing that the neighboring fullback is fast and capable of covering for a mistake. Knowing the nature of their relationship makes the pair stronger.

Be careful not to put your best team in at once if you have to play everybody the same amount. You must determine several good combinations, rather than the best combination, since if the best is on the bench, what does that leave for you to have on the field?

Clearly, the singles/pairs approach is more difficult, if not impossible, to track exactly how much playing time everyone gets. This will require you to find those players who can play multiple positions, since that provides you some extra flexibility in substitutions.

The number of players you have, your ability to manage multiple issues simultaneously, and the sensitivity to equal playing time will determine the substitution method you use. For a travel team, you play the players who give you the best chance of winning, but for house teams you usually must give everyone equal playing time (the equivalent of half the game for everyone).

What Is Next?

The next chapter, "Drills and Positioning," is the heart of this book. It establishes the fundamental activities on the soccer field. After four chapters of primarily off-the-field tasks and some soccer basics, you are ready to start kicking the ball around. However, you still need to do a significant amount of thinking and planning, even as part of drills and positioning.

CHAPTER 5
Drills and Positioning

This is the core chapter of the book as far as soccer on the field. This is the material that other soccer books cover; however, we take a completely different approach with even the traditional soccer content.

We have tried to provide you with lots of useful information in a way that makes it simple for even the novice to make a huge difference as a soccer coach. Additionally, we have included the most effective and advanced techniques that soccer professionals use. The way we do this is to provide a framework of principles that we build upon as we move from peewee through the middle years and then into the tween Years.

The Five Ps of Soccer: Positioning, Psychological, Passing, Physical, and Possession

The Five Ps of Soccer is the framework by which we provide insights into coaching the core soccer skills via drills and positioning activities. Examine the table below; it outlines the evolution of the Five Ps of Soccer and provides some relevant, manageable, and measurable milestones for your coaching endeavors.

Stage	Positioning	Psychological	Passing	Physical	Possession
Peewee	Relative to the ball and goals: go to the line.	Watch the ball and have fun.	Just kick the ball!	N/A	N/A

Stage	Positioning	Psychological	Passing	Physical	Possession
Middle Years	Relative to the ball, goals, and own players.	Game: learn and trust teammates.	Pass to where they should be and to open spaces; understand angles, but just transfer speed in passing (hard feet).	Stretching and stamina are important.	N/A
Tween Years	Relative to ball, goals, own players, and opposition's players.	Sport: learn the subtle aspects of game: soft, low, and slow are better than hard, fast, and high.	Learn multiple types of passes, including crosses, short, long, and loop. Consider where the other team is, not just where your teammates are.	Need to work on core strength and leg strength for power in shooting.	Maintain ball under pressure; soft feet in receiving passes.

The Five Ps of Soccer lay the foundation for many of the drills and positioning tactics.

As everything else that we teach in this book, the skills and methods are cumulative. In later years you will build upon and expand the skills you teach in peewee. However, as you will find out soon, in the middle years, and again in the tween years, you will reteach some techniques that you taught to your peewee players.

For instance, defense changes greatly over the years. In the peewee and middle years, we teach an attack mode (get to the ball quickly). In the tween years, as the opponents get better at controlling the ball, we teach a defender first to get very close to the opponent to cut down passing and dribbling angles, and second to relax and be ready to react to an evasive move. This defensive approach is called pressure and cover.

Discipline: A must for learning

While soccer is supposed to be fun, you must have discipline on the field appropriate for the age group and the clear expectations of behavior at practices and games. Think about the likelihood of your children learning anything in school if other children in class were allowed to talk over the teacher, make noises, or wander around the classroom. There are two types of potential discipline problems: lack of attention and disruptive behavior.

For peewees and players in the middle years, you will likely deal with some inattention from your players. We suggest not getting angry or insisting on peewee players to pay attention. It is your job to make practices interesting enough that they will not be tempted to ignore you. However, at this age they may really not want to be there, so you need to be extremely patient. Do not punish peewee players for lack of attention.

You can minimize behavioral problems by selecting drills where the kids always have a ball at their feet. This limits the opportunity for bad behavior because they are busy and not bored! In addition, it gets them better faster since they actually get more practice (more touches).

However, you must deal with disruptive behavior at any age. Disruptive behavior makes it likely that other players who otherwise would be interested and involved in practice are not. This could be because one player is joking around and in essence being more interesting than you. Do not punish peewee players who are being disruptive; just turn their energy into some other drill. If one player continually talks while you are trying to make a point, then get the disruptor involved. For instance, show the other players how to kick the ball far. Have the disruptor help you by running and getting the ball. You can make it sound as if he is special for getting the opportunity to chase the ball down, but in essence you are wearing the disruptor out and keeping him away from rest of the team until he is too tired to continue being disruptive. Make sure that helping you with the drill is less fun than talking with his friends or doing the drill itself. Otherwise, a player might misbehave just to get the opportunity to assist with a drill.

As you progress into the middle years, you still do not punish children for poor execution. We suggest that you punish children only for lack of respect and disrupting practice. Do not punish by making kids run or do push-ups. Running and push-ups should be seen as part of training, not a punishment. The only acceptable punishment is to sit and do nothing or be sent to parents/home if they will not sit still on their own.

We never punish tweens for poor execution, but at this level we start to develop the ability for children to acknowledge when they have made a mistake. They should always wait for a coach to identify when they need to fix something or perform better. Let them know that they can clap their hands or say "my bad" when they know that they have goofed. There is no need for the coach to say anything.

When coaching in the tween years, if a player disrupts the practice by talking or blatantly not paying attention to the coach or trainer, then send them to the orange cone. Put an orange cone about fifty yards from the practice field. When someone disrespects the team or coach, tell that player to run to the orange cone and back. If you want, have an assistant coach run with the player to ensure he does it with urgency and focus. This is not supposed to be a fun run to avoid some drill, but rather a reminder that he needs to listen during practice. It is important for both children and parents to understand that you, as the coach, cannot put up with disruptive behavior that prevents other attentive children from getting everything possible out of practice.

In summary, the discipline tenets for youth soccer are as follows:

Peewee: Expect players not to disrupt others, but do not expect them to listen to everything. Gently nudge them back into practice or games when they wander.

Middle Years: Expect the kids to be quiet when you are talking, but do not expect them to be riveted on you.

Tweens: The players should know that they will be expected to listen during practice and to acknowledge when they do not execute properly. Disruptive behavior is unacceptable, and the disruptor should be separated from the team temporarily to accentuate the loss of training.

Always start practice on time, even if everyone is not present. Eventually, the players who do not show up on time will start getting there on time. Discipline starts early. Lead by example; lay the foundation for your players that they will get out of soccer what they put into it. If your players practice with lack of attention and purpose, then their lack of improvement in soccer skills will reflect their poor commitment. In addition, if they do not practice hard, then likely they will not play hard.

Positioning

Many coaches focus largely on ballhandling skills from the early levels of soccer, but we think positioning is equally as important as ballhandling skills. The balance between individual skills and team play is out of whack for youth soccer. You must make teamwork as the top priority, and to do that you must emphasize where the players should be located relative to their teammates, the field, and their opposition. How well they control the ball is important once they are in the right place, but if they are in the wrong place it will not matter how well they can dribble or pass.

Experimentation

Experimenting is crucial. The sooner you encourage your players to take risks with the ball on the field, the more they will learn and the faster they will learn it. Allow your players to make mistakes early and often. This experience will pay off later.

Teach decision making

Do not focus too much on rigid rules, but rather emphasize free-flowing, controlled soccer. As stated earlier, never say "never," but provide the kids the power to make decisions based upon all of the information available to them on the field. Do not coach from play to play, but rather discuss after the fact what worked and what did not work. Since you know what they will probably do wrong, do not stop them from making a mistake, but rather see if they can figure out a solution without being told. Players will learn this lesson faster and permanently if you allow them to make mistakes, rather than if you tell them what to do each play. You cannot learn for them. The best you can do is to give them the *opportunity* to learn.

Cones? Do you see any cones on the soccer field during a game?

Do away with drills where cones are part of the activity. Only use cones to mark playing areas, divide the field, or as a point of reference.

"Do you see any cones on the soccer field during a soccer game? I do not!" The kids love to hear us rant about this. If you want to use cones for part of a drill, use an assistant coach or parent. These "cones" can even talk and move, if you need them to. For the more intellectual coaches, kids, and parents, we call them our cognitive cones. This also provides a way for you to involve more people in the practice.

At the peewee level, cognitive cones can say, "Good job," or, "Way to go." They provide encouragement while the children are practicing.

For players in the middle years, cognitive cones can provide some resistance, defensing, encouragement, and simple coaching. These coaches learn more about the strengths and weaknesses of the players, so they can make some insightful suggestions to you about where certain players should play or skills the team needs to work on.

Cognitive cones who share the field with tween players may need to wear shin guards or be tough, because they might get bumped during contact drills. This type of interaction can measurably add to the intensity of the practice. However, you need to ensure that these grown-ups do not hurt any of your players.

Practice Schedules

Before we discuss specific drills, let's examine what an overall practice is likely to include for each age group.

For Peewee: A typical practice is forty-five minutes long, held once or twice a week. Break it down as follows:

- Ten minutes of warm-ups
- Ten minutes of dribbling drills
- Twenty-five minutes of positioning drills and scrimmaging

The goal of peewee practice is to get the children comfortable with each other and the flow of the game.

For the Middle Years: Schedule two practices a week, one instructional practice and one scrimmage practice. A typical drill practice is sixty minutes long and should be broken down as follows:

- Ten minutes of warm-ups. Have your players do the triangle drill as they show up.
- Twenty minutes of dribbling and passing drills
- Twenty minutes of tackling and contact drills
- Ten minutes of shooting drills

A typical scrimmage practice is sixty minutes long and should be run as follows:

- Ten to fifteen minutes of warm-ups. Have your players do the triangle drill as they show up.
- Forty-five minutes of instructional scrimmaging

Instructional scrimmaging is a fantastic drill because it works on stamina, decision making, and reinforcing the drills learned at the previous drill practice. For the first twenty to thirty minutes of the instructional scrimmage, you should stop the scrimmage to provide positive reinforcement and identify critical flaws. Always stop more for positive comments than for negative comments.

Let the players run without interruption the last fifteen to twenty-five minutes of the scrimmage, much like a real game. Do not stop the play; rather, discuss issues at a break or pull out a single player to discuss objectives while the scrimmage continues. This usually requires that you have several other coaches helping you so that you can focus on an individual player or an individual situation, while ensuring that the rest of the scrimmage has adult supervision.

If other players are watching the scrimmage, ask them questions about what is going on out on the field. Use every activity to teach them to think through the complexities of the game. You cannot be out there with them, so your players need to learn to make good, quick decisions on their own. Kids start by making slow, incorrect decisions, but they will improve if you let them practice making decisions.

Give yourself five minutes at the end of the scrimmage to discuss what trends you saw, and ask the kids what they thought they did well and what aspects they believe they need to work on.

For Tween Years: Tweens usually just have two practices a week, but they run ninety minutes each. We suggest that you have one instructional practice and one scrimmage practice per week.

Run a typical instructional practice as follows:

• Ten to fifteen minutes of warm-ups and stretching
• Twenty to twenty-five minutes of ballhandling skills, agility, and speed training

Ballhandling skills are vital. Agility eventually translates into speed, and speed is both physical and mental. When a ball is played into space as a situation, an agile and sound player will be able to get there, twisting and turning to be in a good defensive position to win the ball or an offensive position to control the situation.

• Twenty to twenty-five minutes of complex drills (scenarios)

These lay the foundation for the scrimmage, which follows. Spend this time working on different scenarios consistent with the focus for the week. You will find scenarios later in this chapter.

• Thirty to forty minutes of instructional scrimmaging

Let your team play and encourage them to make their own decisions—but good ones—and to take things they learned from the scenarios into the scrimmage. Learning soccer is all about repetition. If only a quarter of the kids understand the objective of the scenarios and translate it into better play in a game situation, you are making progress.

The scrimmage practice for tweens should be run as follows:

Start with fifteen minutes of warm-ups before you scrimmage for the rest of the time. Warm-ups may include running laps or doing soccer drills. Keep in mind that warm-ups for tweens must be of higher intensity and longer than for players in the middle years. Their muscles are getting more developed, and lack of a proper warm-up could lead to an injury in this age group.

To enhance stamina, we suggest that each time you substitute a player into the scrimmage, the player coming out of the scrimmage should sprint around the field once before waiting on the bench to be put back in the scrimmage.

An alternative way to conduct a ninety-minute instructional practice for tweens is:

• Fifteen minutes of warm-ups and stretching
• Ten minutes of drills focused on one skill, such as shooting, passing, heading, and dribbling
• Twenty minutes of ballhandling skills, speed, and agility
• Forty-five minutes of instructional scrimmaging, with the first twenty minutes performing scenarios (with lots of stopping and teaching), followed by twenty-five minutes of free playing (with no stopping)

Have a plan

The key is not to pick one of these practices necessarily but rather to have a plan and be consistent. At this age, kids are comfortable with and learn best in a well-defined, repeatable practice. They need boundaries. Variety in practice can come from your awareness of their improvement in the details of soccer and your enthusiasm, not necessarily from a multitude of drills.

Drills: Quality over Quantity

Instead of grouping and explaining hundreds of drills by the specific skills they improve, we have chosen a few drills and grouped them into foundation activities, basic skills, and complex drills, or scenarios. As a result, we provide a minimum of items for you to learn while providing the maximum benefit to your team and players.

Foundation activities are drills that you start to use in the peewee years. However, they are flexible enough to add complexity and difficulty over time to make them appropriate as your team moves through the stages of youth soccer. Try to use five to eight drills each season, with half being foundation activities that are augmented from the season before. Our focus on quality over quantity minimizes the number of drills that you are expected to learn and pass on to your team. As a result, you will do a better job coaching and your players will do a better job learning the skills.

Basic skills focus on drills that are task-specific, such as shooting, throw-ins, and heading. Use these in addition to the foundation activities during the middle years.

The tween years require even more complex drills, or scenarios. The following figure depicts how the drills combine to provide the portfolio of drills for each age group.

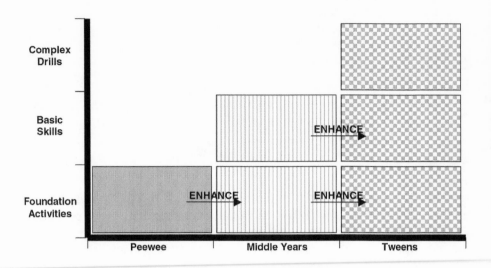

Foundation Activities

1. Sprints Plus
2. The Rope
3. Triangle Drill
4. Sharks and Minnows
5. Basic Shooting

Basic Skills

1. Stiff Leg (tackling and possession)
2. Cross (shooting)
3. The Weave (passing and shooting)
4. Fence Fury (foot strike)
5. Heading Circle (heading)
6. Softie (trapping)
7. Throw-ins
8. Juggling (volleying and trapping)

Complex Drills (Scenarios)

1. 3v3/3v2 Counterattack
2. 2v2

3. 3v2 Offense vs. Defense
4. Bread and Butter
5. 4v4 Small-Sided Game

Foundation Activities

Foundation activities are enhanced at each age group and continue to be an important component of practice from peewee through the tween years. Players in the middle years still use foundation activities, but practices focus on the basic skills. Similarly, by the tween years, the complex drills, or scenarios, are the focus of most practices. This is especially true if you have been able to keep your team together, so that each year is a cumulative process. However, for the house teams, you need to be prepared to get new players every season.

1. Sprints Plus

A simple sprint across the field without the ball is the foundation for both warm-ups and ballhandling skills. The following sequence is very productive, and you can mix it up with an infinite number of variations.

Line up your players along one sideline with their soccer ball pushed slightly behind them. Tell your team that on the whistle, they need to sprint to the other sideline. You can have them do a variety of things at the other end. You may have them turn around immediately, do five push-ups, or line up again.

As coaches, we often run with our teams. We like to say that we do not ask them to do anything that we would not do.

Once they are back to the sideline with their balls and you think that they have loosened up enough or you have made your point about running, have them put their soccer ball on the sideline in front of them.

You have many ways in which to proceed from here. We normally start the players on the whistle and have them dribble the ball to the other sideline. When they get to the other sideline, they stop the ball *on* the sideline. We may ask them to use only their left foot or alternate between using their left foot and right foot. You can later expand this drill by having them use the outside of their feet to dribble the ball down the field. Using the outside of their feet in dribbling is another critical skill that will pay great dividends later, so start them doing this in the middle years. Notice that there are no cones for these fundamental drills. This permits you to go from one activity to another without wasting time picking up cones.

Later, you may ask the players to do all of this dribbling while yelling out how many fingers you are holding up. You should run backwards, while they come toward you, changing the number of fingers once everyone has yelled it out. The children love this because they get to scream and holler. (Sometimes, they even get to see the coach either stumble or fall.) This drill helps them learn to on dribble with their head up, an important skill. Once kids have learned to dribble while watching the ball at their feet, it is very difficult to break them of the habit. That's why we do this drill for the peewees too.

We emphasize dribbling with the outside of the foot as players get into the middle years because it provides an option for more-controlled and precise dribbling and passing. I like to get down real low and whisper to the kids that this is our secret weapon: "The other kids only have two feet each, but when we use the outside of our feet it is like we have four feet. What a deal!"

Devin (in the light jersey) is dribbling the ball with the outside of her foot. This permits her to dribble the ball in the same direction as her foot is moving and often throws off her opponent.

Dribbling this way allows kids to pass to the right with their right foot. Think about that: the defender is usually thinking that the right foot swings to the left.

In the middle years, this technique can provide an advantage in the open field. It is equally useful for dribbling around a defender.

You can also have the players do a drill at the other sideline once they get done so that the faster kids do not get bored. You may have them do the stair stepper, where they put one foot on top of the ball and then in one movement put the other foot on top of the ball while the other foot returns to the ground. They should do the stair stepper while spinning around the ball. This activity gets them used to controlling the ball and gauging how high the ball is. This awareness is essential for judging where to put their feet when they start to trap the ball later or receive passes from their teammates.

Once your players have gone back and forth several times using a variety of dribbling techniques by themselves, you should put a few coaches on the field to exert pressure on the players as they dribble across the field. Teach them to dribble around the pressure on the backside of the defender. As a defender approaches, the player should dribble to the side of the defender that their backside is pointing, since it will require the defender to rotate his body to get a foot on the ball.

If it is difficult to tell which way the defender's backside is pointing, your players should dribble to the side of the defender where their foot is closer to the dribbler. Going around the defender is so much easier when the kids dribble with both the inside and outside of their feet, since it provides the option of planting with the foot, which in turn provides the most lateral movement to evade a defender. If your players use only the inside of their foot, they have to bring the ball all the way across their body; and since the defender is probably marking up on their body, that defender will be better positioned to take the ball.

Once the kids are worn out by running back and forth working against defensive pressure (or the coaches are pooped out), have them pair up and pass the ball back and forth going sideline to sideline. Instruct them to pass to where their teammate *should be*, not to where they *are*. This idea of leading their teammate will take time and practice, but always emphasize that it is better to pass too far ahead of a teammate than behind him. Once the players have the hang of passing the ball back and forth without any pressure, put the assistant coaches back on the field and apply gentle defensive pressure.

This entire sequence of sprints plus can amount to half of the drill practices for players in the middle year. You can make this drill progressively harder by adding more pressure from coaches, as well as more repetitions and more stringent requirements for crisper passing. The ultimate drill of passing down the field under defensive pressure prepares them well for game situations. As players approach the tween years, they will have to be able to settle the ball and back pass or change fields. However, for the first few years of youth soccer, your goal should be to get them to reliably move the ball down the field.

2. The Rope

Young players are not allowed to cross the street on their own because they do not have good enough depth perception. It isn't their fault; their brains cannot process the information accurately. Yet we hear coaches yelling out at soccer matches for their players to keep their spacing. So how do we expect this magic to occur on the soccer field?

At the peewee level, you must have the kids think about only the ball and the goal. Do not complicate their positioning with anything else. To do this, use a physical prop such as a ten-to twenty-yard-long rope. You can this rope in a variety of ways during the peewee and middle years.

For peewee players, use the rope to identify the most likely path that a player with the ball will take toward a goal.

The diagram below shows the situation when the opponent is coming toward the goal and shows how your players should react. Direct them to "go to the imaginary line" between the ball and their goal and then attack the ball.

Keep the direction and the objectives simple. This is when you begin to teach the critical axiom that *what you do without the ball is more important than what you do with the ball*. The diagram shows only four players at once. If you get too many more it becomes very chaotic, so have another coach do the same thing at the other goal, or have your players working with another coach on another drill at the same time. This is also the number of players you normally have on a field at once during a peewee match.

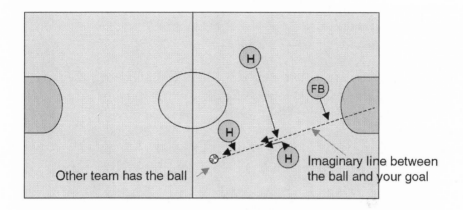

If you want to avoid "magnet ball" and lay the foundation for smart soccer players, you must get your team to "go to the imaginary line" rather than chase the ball around the field.

Of course, the ball will be moving continually as the other team tries to score. As a result, your team will never get lined up on the imaginary line. However, it is important that your players understand the purpose of going to the line: if a player is between his own goal and the ball, then it is less likely that the other team will be able to score. In addition, he will be in a better position to take the ball away, since he will be where the other team is going. Conversely, if he follows the ball around the field, then he will be where the other team just was.

This concept is nearly impossible for the kids to get without a visual aid. So this is when you use the rope drill. Get a coach to hold one end of the rope in the middle of the goal. You hold the other end and move around the field. Have the kids run to the rope and then run toward you. Do not try to move around once the kids have arrived at the rope; otherwise, they will be tripping all over the place. Once you think that they get the idea, then set aside the rope and have them go to the imaginary line without the rope. You can start to speed up and move around with the ball as the final level of difficulty.

Your objective here is to get your players to start to understand angles. This is an elusive skill, but highly useful for your team to possess. It requires a special trait in a talented player to stop another player from scoring by intercepting the opponent at just the last moment. This happens in football games. Often some fast kickoff returner is sprinting down the sideline, and then an opponent comes sprinting into view and knocks the kickoff returner out of bounds. The tackler did not run toward the player; he ran to where that player would be and met him there.

The concept of the imaginary line is also relevant for when your team has the ball, except it is the opposite. On offense, if your players do not have the ball, they should stay away from the line. The diagram below depicts this scenario.

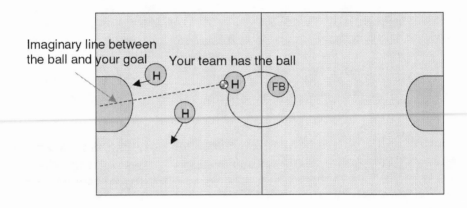

While on offense, peewee players should find and then avoid the imaginary line to provide the best opportunity for their teammate with the ball.

Your players need to avoid the line as if it were hot or dangerous. Have fun with this drill. Once the ball is closer to the opponent's goal than your player is, then he runs toward the goal. If he is off the line and watching the ball, then he will be available for a pass or to get a rebound from an attempted shot.

Note that in the figure above, the fullback does not stand back by his own goal. The fullback should move up as far as the halfway line and think of themselves as the last person who can stop the goal. Therefore, he should stay on that imaginary line between the ball and his own goal, even when the ball is way down the field. This ensures that he will slow down the oncoming player and not just follow the opponent down the field. Fullbacks will use this alignment all the way through the middle years, so this is a good foundation.

As an engineer and physics professor, I understood geometry but not soccer. Therefore, I was confused as to how these young kids could keep their spacing when coming down the field as a team. So I pulled out the rope used in peewee for the "go to the imaginary line" drill and handed one end to each of two of my players. I tossed a ball out in front of them, pointed to the other goal eighty yards away, and told them to pass the ball back and forth down the field without letting the rope touch the ground. After a few giggles and trips, the players got the idea of spacing.

Do this drill without too many other players around because it is easy for them to trip one another on the field. A few eighty-yard sessions with the rope are quite useful in getting players to understand *how* to keep their spacing. If they kick the ball a little short, then they know to move away from the ball. If they pass a bit long, they know that they have to speed up a bit to keep the same distance from the player receiving the ball, who must accelerate to get the long ball.

3. Triangle Drill

This is our favorite simple drill, which is so easy to make more difficult as your players get older. Arrange three players in an equilateral triangle; for peewee players should stand about five yards apart. Have them pass the ball in turn around the triangle to each other.

For peewee, all you want is for the players to keep the ball moving. Do not worry about form or speed for at this level. The focus should be on repetition and confidence. Your young players will experiment and get the ball to their teammates.

Once they can do this, ask your peewee players to do two things: use the inside of their feet and use both feet. If you can train your peewee players to get comfortable striking the ball with either foot, you will be way ahead of most teams. Do not expect most players at this level to do both tasks well. However, you can gently mention what is the right way to play. Young children are smarter than you think. Do not press the players to perform these skills expertly, but introduce the skills to all of the players. Some of the kids will start to pick up on the advanced techniques.

In the middle years, the triangle drill is a treasure trove of opportunities to reinforce critical soccer lessons. For instance, you can move the players farther apart, up to ten to twenty yards. Make sure the spacing between the players in the triangle stays the same. As passes are made several yards to one side of the receiving player, that player will have to move to the ball. In turn, the other two players must react to the player going after the ball by keeping the triangle equilateral. This reinforces that what you do without the ball is more important than what you do with the ball.

Simultaneously, you can work on a couple of different ballhandling skills in tandem with the triangle drill. The first skill is one touch, in which the players pass to the other players with a single touch. This pass is good to learn for fast-moving games. The second skill is the trap-carry pass, in which players trap the pass with the foot nearest where the pass is coming from, carry it to the other foot (moving a few feet in the process), and then pass to the other player using the other foot. The trap-carry pass is useful for situations where the receiving player has to avoid an opponent to make a good pass.

The last major addition to the triangle drill used for the middle years is to put a defender in the middle of the triangle. The primary objective of this variation of the drill is to work on your players' ability to make decisions about the best teammate to pass to and how to get open for a pass from a teammate.

At first, it is best to have an assistant coach play the defender in the middle of the triangle. The coach will overplay to one of the two players without the ball. In doing this, the coach hopes to see two things. First, the player being shadowed by the defender should move to keep a passing lane between him and the player with the ball. We often talk about how a player's mother or father uses this same technique in a busy mall. If the parent cannot see his child, then that means the child is in the wrong place. Similarly, if a defender comes between you and your teammate with the ball, the person without the ball must move to get open (create a situation where the player with the ball can see you).

Second, the coach should observe that the player with the ball passes to the teammate who is most open. The defender should move around just like a defender would in a game, thus requiring the player with the ball to keep his head up and be aware of where all players are. As the defender gets the passer and other players to adjust to the defensive attack, you must remind the players to move without the ball and maintain spacing that provides the optimum opportunity for passes between the three players in the triangle.

Putting a player in the middle of the triangle as the defender turns the game into a small competition. If the defender intercepts the ball, then the person who made the errant pass becomes the defender and the defender becomes part of the triangle. This is a great way to teach players about angles and anticipating other players' actions..

In the tween years, all of the aspects of the triangle drill hold the same potential for learning, but you'll need to add some new twists to challenge your more advanced players. One idea is to put two defenders in the triangle. This requires the receiving players to work much harder and makes the decisions by the passer much more difficult. You also can require that the triangle, with a defender inside, move from one goal to the next and have one of the players take a shot on goal at the end.

4. Sharks and Minnows

Sharks and minnows is a classic drill that children never seem to tire of, perhaps because there are so many ways to make it more interesting and competitive with just a little imagination. The primary objective of this activity is to get the minnows to dribble the ball and protect it from an opponent. Simultaneously, the sharks work on attacking the ball and figuring out the angles to close in on an opponent with the ball. In addition, this drill is a great way to keep everybody busy and work on stamina to some extent.

The drill is started by defining an area on the field and having all of your players, except for one or two, get in that area with their soccer ball. The area may be the circle at the middle of the field, or you can have four coaches or cones make a square area. The players in the area with their soccer balls are called the minnows and will soon be attacked by the shark(s). Depending on how quickly you want to clear out the minnows, you may start with one or two sharks.

The objective is for the shark(s) to try to get a minnow's soccer ball out of the defined area by kicking it away from him or by forcing him to dribble it out of the area trying to avoid the shark(s).

After a minnow has his ball knocked out of the area, you have several options. You may have the minnow become a shark. This makes the game go much faster, since very soon there are more sharks than minnows—so the balls get knocked out quickly. You can then designate the last one or two minnows that were able to survive the onslaught of sharks as the starting sharks for the next round.

Another option for the defeated minnows is for them to watch and cheer on their fellow minnows. This is an interesting approach, since it creates a situation where the weaker players might be watching how the better players are able to avoid getting their ball taken away—a great byproduct of the drill. Yet another option is tell the players who leave the area because their ball was knocked out by a shark to do some task, such as dribble around the area, until all minnows are knocked out. This maintains constant activity, but also becomes quite chaotic.

Whichever way you use this drill, do not be afraid to be creative and try new approaches to making it interesting. For example, my U11 girls team asked to do sharks and minnows in a practice. I decided that when they were knocked out by a shark, they had to juggle their soccer ball until all minnows were eliminated.

Sharks and minnows can get very physical as your kids move through the middle years and into the tween years. This is especially true if you end up with two evenly matched players at the end.

A way to make sharks and minnows more difficult and interesting in the tween years is to allow the defeated minnows to line the perimeter of the playing area and be able to receive a pass from any surviving minnow inside to help avoid having the ball knocked out by a shark. The outside minnow must immediately pass the ball back to the inside minnow. This variation provides several more decision-making options for the minnow, which is the objective of drills.

5. Basic Shooting

At the peewee level, there is little need to practice shooting the soccer ball since the kids will basically dribble the ball into the goal. However, running a simple drill in which your players can experiment with how the ball moves when they hit it at different points in their stride will help them move from dribbling the ball into the goal to shooting it.

Lay the same rope that you have used for the rope drill on the ground about five yards in front of the goal. Start your team, one at a time, from the halfway line by passing them the ball. Have them dribble directly to the goal but shoot the ball as soon as they cross the rope. You can move the rope closer or farther from the goal in order to make the shooting more or less difficult.

At this age we do not suggest that you work real hard on the foot strike. However, you should at least show your players that while they pass the ball with the side of their foot, they shoot the ball by striking it just to the left of their laces (if they are right-footed), on the big bone of the foot. Conversely, if your players are left-footed, they should strike the ball just to the right of their laces. Emphasize to your players that they should not strike the ball with the toes of their cleats. Show them how hitting the ball with their toe makes it really hard to determine where the ball goes.

Each time after they have shot the ball, the players should retrieve it and dribble back to you (or an assistant coach) at the halfway line and then repeat the process. The area around the goal will get very chaotic, but that is okay. Each player will be touching the ball, and they will be having fun dodging and kicking at the balls.

The most important objective of this drill is to get the kids to work on the proper form of kicking the ball hard (shooting it) versus kicking the ball just hard enough to keep it in front of them (dribbling it).

Loving the ball

As your team progresses from peewee to the middle years, you must help players fall in love with the soccer ball. Their ballhandling skills will never fully develop until they are comfortable with the ball at their feet. As a physics professor, I often told my students that studying physics should be dangerous to their roommates. Similarly, playing soccer should be slightly irritating to your players' parents. The kids should shuffle around the house with the soccer ball, roll it under their feet at dinner, kick the ball around in the yard, and maybe even toss it into their bed at night.

Our culture offers so many distractions for our children that appear to be more interesting than playing with a soccer ball, such as watching television and playing computer games. But around the world, many kids return home from school and the first thing they do is juggle, dribble, or generally play with their soccer ball when left alone. Encourage your players to see the soccer ball as a constant companion, and they will make up games with it that will eventually make them more comfortable with the ball on the field.

Basic Skills

The seven basic skills that follow start to provide specific training for behavior needed in a full 8v8 game. Many of these work well for warm-ups for before games, as well as for drills during practices.

1. Stiff Leg (tackling and possession)
2. Cross (shooting)
3. The Weave (passing and shooting)
4. Fence Fury (foot strike)
5. Heading Circle (heading)
6. Softie (trapping)
7. Throw-ins
8. Juggling (volleying)

These skills are very simple, so we provide few diagrams as a result. You know when you have done a skill right when the players are having fun and using what they have learned in practice in the games. This overall process is nothing fancy: learn, practice, execute in game, and repeat.

1. Stiff Leg (tackling and possession)

Players line up about ten yards from a coach with their soccer ball. They dribble a couple of steps to the coach and then pass it right to the coach. The coach traps and controls the ball while the player advances toward the coach and firmly kicks the ball from the coach. In doing so, the player must gets his hips over the ball, keep the attacking leg stiff, stay under control, and, hopefully, knock the ball from the coach. The ball should not go flying away; rather, the player should shove the ball *through* the coach and then leave, having the ball under his control.

You may do this with one coach, but then it conflicts with our preferred criteria of not having a drill where the players stand in line. The best way to do this drill is with three to four coaches spaced fifteen yards apart so that the players, once started, never stop.

2. Cross (shooting)

Place a coach at each goalpost and have two lines of players at the corner of the 18 yard line. The coach on the right goalpost passes the ball to the first player on the left side, who takes one tap to settle the ball and then shoots. He chases the ball down if he misses and exits around the left side, while the coach on the left goalpost passes the ball to the first player on the right side, which proceeds at full speed to shoot on the goal, and so on.

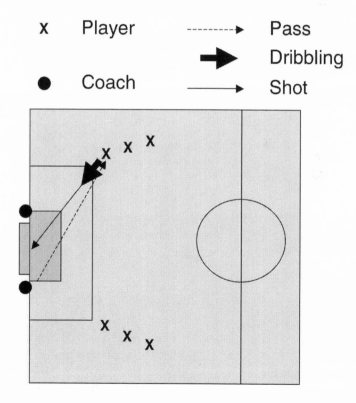

The cross drill is a great activity for working on first touch, attacking, and shooting.

The figure above shows the cross drill sequence from one side. Once the goalkeeper has set up again and the shooter has cleared the area, the coach on the other side passes to the other corner of the 18 yard line. This alternating sequence continues for ten minutes, until you sense that it is time to start another drill or you think that they have mastered the shooting from this angle.

The players shooting must hustle around the back of the goal (get some running in) and go to the other side (to get work on shooting from both sides). The emphasis on this drill is for players to look where the goalkeeper is, shoot where the goalkeeper is not, make a solid foot strike, and follow their shots. Do not let your players run around their non-dominant foot (usually their left foot). Running around their non-dominant foot means to avoid shooting or trapping with that foot because it is weaker. If they run around their weak side, it will provide the other team much more time to defend against your player. The ability to shoot the ball with both feet is a key difference between an average player and a good player in the middle years.

3. The Weave (passing and shooting)

The weave progresses as shown in the figure below. The players line up on the halfway line in three lines with all of the soccer balls in front of the middle line.

The purpose of the weave is to practice passing, moving without the ball, shooting, and following s teammate's shot. As you players in the middle years perform this drill for the first time, look for energy and the ball ending up in the net.

The drill is started by the middle line (Player X1) taking one touch (the player receives the ball and passes it all in one motion) and then passing downfield to the first player in either the left or the right line. The figure below shows the right line (Player X2) receiving the first pass. The person passing then runs behind the person he passed to. The person receiving the ball then takes two to three touches, while moving diagonally down the field, and passes to the third remaining player (Player X3). Player X2 then loops behind Player X3. This continues until the person receiving the ball is close enough to take a shot. The other players need to follow the shot and crash on the goal to put in deflections or rebounds from the original shot.

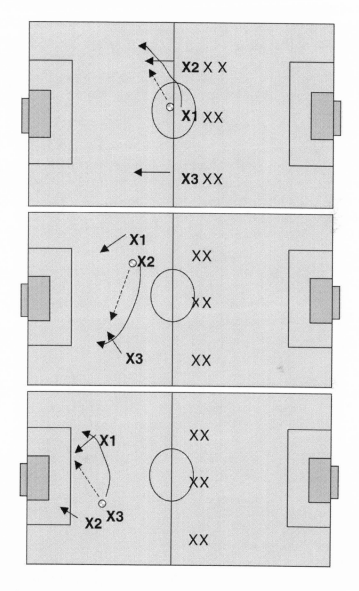

The weave drill works on passing, positioning, shooting, and stamina.

The three players who just completed the drill should retrieve their ball and go back into different lines than where they started. They should return to midfield by running back outside of the passing area, so as not to get in the way of the next wave of players coming down the field. It is important to keep the intensity level up. In this drill players do not stand in line very long, so stress to them that they need to run, not walk, back to their place in line.

While learning skills is essential, it is even more important to ensure that your players can execute near 100 percent when they are tired. If executed properly, this can be a very tiring drill.

This drill teaches many aspects important to soccer, and you can make it increasingly demanding between the middle and tween years. Remind players in the middle years that they are to pass to where their teammate should be, not to where he is. This drill should help your players gauge the speed of teammates and how much to lead them for a pass. The looping action behind the player they pass to reinforces the concept of making space on the field. This should be done at full game speed, which adds to the aerobic aspect of this drill.

The amount of dribbling you allow can make this drill very easy or very hard. When first running this drill, let your players take as many touches necessary to settle the ball before they pass it. However, you can push your team by making this a one-touch drill: each player is required to use a one-touch pass each time.

As your team gets comfortable with this drill, you can put two goalkeepers in the net and have them just push the ball back out to ensure that there is a deflection. This will encourage the non-shooting players (and the shooter) to follow the shot. Having a single coach or defender in the middle of the field can disrupt the rhythm of this drill, but it also provides a more realistic game situation for the players.

4. Fence Fury (foot strike)

In the basic shooting activity, we described where the player should strike ball with his cleats. However, several other parts of the body must be considered when shooting, as these four major features of a good, strong foot strike demonstrate:

- The foot that is not kicking the ball (the plant foot) should be very close (three to four inches, or one hand-width maximum) to the ball.
- The leg of the kicking foot should be bent and the knee above the ball.

- The foot that is striking the ball should be pointed so that the top of the foot can hit the middle of the ball as it swings through the ball.
- After striking the ball, the kicking leg must follow through and the toe remain pointed. The ball usually goes where the plant foot is pointing and/ or the toe of the kicking foot ends up pointing.

The picture on the cover of the book shows good form going into a shot. Notice how Grace is looking at the ball and her arms are also rotating to help with the leg kick, which propels the ball toward the goal.

In order to make a simple foot strike drill interesting, but also efficient, get two to three assistant coaches to help you with the drill. This drill can get incrementally more challenging in the middle and tween years by following this progression.

For players in the middle years, start by finding a chain link fence and have your players all line up side by side, separated by at least five feet, about three to four feet away from the fence but facing it. The players repeatedly practice the foot strike by kicking the ball against the chain link fence while you and the assistant coaches walk up and down the line of players providing encouragement and reminders about basic form. Do not worry about accuracy or speed at first. Just focus on form. Keep your players pretty close to the fence to begin with, since the typical problem is that they will kick the ball up into the air. If they get too far from the fence, they will be spending a lot of time running around and retrieving their soccer ball. In addition, by staying closer to the fence, they get more kicks in since they do not have as far to walk to get their soccer ball back.

The next challenge is to use either foot to shoot. Each player usually has a dominant foot. However, one of your primary jobs early in youth soccer coaching is for you to work hard to break your players of this tendency. So have them take an equal number of shots with their left foot as they do with their right foot. It will not be pretty at first, but be patient and just worry about form.

The next aspect of shooting is for the players to get a feel for where on the ball they should strike it to make the ball stay low or go high. We suggest that you move the kids to about ten to fifteen feet away from the fence and then have them aim for a point about two to three feet off of the ground to hit the fence. The lower on the ball your players strike it, the higher the ball goes, and vice versa.

You can make a game of this by having the kids line up about fifteen to twenty feet in front of a coach. Preferably, use several coaches to create several shooting galleries going at once. While the coach holds a hand at different locations, you challenge the kids to shoot the ball to hit the coach's hand. If they hit the hand of the coach, the coach does ten push-ups. Or, you keep track of the total number of hits, and the winning group gets to pick the next drill. Regardless, use some form of motivation to make the drill more interesting.

Finally, look for the players' ability to shoot the ball and without spinning it. A quick physics lesson will explain why this is important. If a player can generate only a certain amount of kinetic energy (related to speed) by kicking the ball, you want as much of that energy as possible to go into moving the ball forward and into the net for the game-winning score. However, if the ball is spinning around, then some of the energy that your player gave the ball is wasted in the spinning of the ball, rather than moving the ball faster toward the goal.

Challenge your players to strike the ball without making it spin. As the kids experiment, they will find the sweet spot, where the foot strike produces the minimum amount of spinning. The lack of spin occurs when the foot hits the middle of the ball, plus the plant foot and toe of the kicking foot are pointing in the same direction. This combination is difficult to draw up in a diagram, but suffice it say that if players take fifty shots with each foot and they pay attention to how the strike of the foot feels in relation to the spin of the ball, they will start to feel the best motion to get this effect. This is when a good trainer, who has played a high level of soccer, is very useful since he has mastered the more subtle techniques of footstrike and field tactics.

You likely will not use this drill much in the tween years because you will want your players on the field with the goal so you can measure their accuracy relative to the goal. However, when a goal is not available, going back to this drill and working on placement is always useful. Be careful, though; the older kids kick pretty hard, so back them up a bit more for your own safety.

5. Heading Circle (heading)

Heading the ball (striking the ball with the head) can be worrisome to young children, so you need to start slowly on the headers. That is why we do not recommend trying these drills with peewee players.

When having your children head the ball, make sure that they strike the ball with their hairline, not their nose (that hurts) and not the top of their heads (they will never be able to direct the ball). Their little heads will get sore pretty quickly, so do not do more than ten minutes at a time of any header drill.

The primary way to get started on headers is to play head catch with the team. Have the players arrange themselves in a circle around you, and then toss the ball to each player in turn at head height. Say either, "Head!" or, "Catch!" when you toss the ball. The player needs to do the *opposite*. This is really funny to watch the first few times. If you say "catch," the player heads the ball back to you. If the player does the wrong act, then he is eliminated. Have the eliminated players do jumping jacks, juggling, or push-ups while the competition continues to keep them active. Keep tossing the ball until all but one player is eliminated. The last player is the winner. There usually is no need to reward your players for such a simple activity; they respond to the challenge of being the last one standing.

An alternative heading drill that provides more activity follows begins by pairing up your players. One player kneels and his partner stands in front of him with a ball in hand. Explain to the children the proper heading technique, which is that right before the ball is thrown, they must lock their neck muscles, arch their back slightly, and then move forward into the ball as it is thrown and head it back to their partner. They can do ten headers, then change places with their partners. To make it a bit competitive, they can keep track of how many times they were able to head the ball right back into their partner's hands.

After everyone can do headers reliably from their knees, have them stand up and use the same techniques. Once they have mastered performing headers from the standing position, have them jump up to make contact with the headers. Keep going with this progression until they are either exhausted or have made some progress.

6. Softie (trapping)

Trapping is controlling a ball that is moving through the air. This is an important skill in order to run an offense with precision or play a solid defense.

Before starting the drill, demonstrate to your players how to catch an "egg" so it doesn't break. Throw the ball high in the air, and as it comes down stick your hands high up to catch it. As it hits your hands, bring your hands slowly down to stop the momentum and lessen the impact.

Next, explain to your players that whenever they approach a ball that is played into their feet, they first should bring their foot forward to receive the ball, and as their foot makes contact with, they should keep bringing their foot back to slow the ball's momentum to a complete stop.

If you are the only coach, split the kids up and let half play a small-sided game while you work with the other half. This way the kids don't stand around in a line doing nothing. Set a starting point or line and let the kids get in line. About fifteen feet away, set up a small square area (three yards by three yards or four yards by four yards) with cones. On your command, and in turn, each child has to run toward the area as the coach plays the ball into the area, and the player must trap the ball without it going out of the area. The player then pulls the ball back, dribbles it to the next player in line, high-fives that player, pulls the ball back again, and passes the ball to the coach. Then the next player goes.

You can make it even more fun by having your players shoot at a goal. Any player who doesn't keep the ball in the area on the trap loses the opportunity to shoot on goal. After a short series, where each player goes through about four to five times, you rotate and work with the other group.

If other coaches are helping, you can split the team up into several groups and have all of them work on the drill at the same time. As the players get more and more comfortable throughout the year, keep shrinking the size of the trapping area.

7. Throw-ins

Throw-ins are gradually introduced in youth soccer. They are not used in peewee leagues at all. In the middle years, referees will usually let almost any throw-in count, while in the tween years players are expected to perform throw-ins correctly.

As with many other drills, we suggest using a results-oriented drill that you can make into a competition. Have your team line up along the sideline of the soccer field, facing the middle of the field. Each player throws the ball as far as he can. Then, while the balls are still on the field, have assistant coaches note which ball traveled the farthest. The player who has the longest throw-in is awarded one point. Once that player has been identified, have each player sprint to his ball, then dribble it to the other sideline. Once on the other sideline, the players get ready for the next throw-in, back to the center of the field. This sequence proceeds until one player has reached ten points. That player gets a round of applause from rest of the team, or you can pull out a Gatorade for the winner from your coach's bag.

While you conduct this drill, make sure that the players are doing the throw-in correctly. There are only two essential factors to keep in mind for throw-ins. First, the player must grab the ball with both hands and raise the ball behind his head, then throw the ball straight ahead. The second critical aspect of the throw-in is that both feet must stay on the ground. Normally, a player's back foot comes off the ground when performing a throw-in. The harder he tries to throw the ball in, the more likely his back foot will come off of the ground. The best way to prevent this from happening is to instruct the player to *drag* the back foot. Your players should exaggerate this *dragging* effect until they get comfortable doing throw-ins.

8. Juggling (volleying)

Many people don't understand the concept of juggling. Soccer players don't juggle just to look cool keeping the ball up in the air or treat it like a trick they perform to impress others. Juggling improves players' ability to control a ball passed to them in the air. In addition, juggling builds up their confidence. The ability to juggle directly translates into a player's ability to volley the ball. Volleying is when the player strikes the ball with his foot while the ball is in the air.

Soccer is a Thinking Game

In the 1986 FIFA World Cup, Diego Maradona's Argentina squad won the championship and Maradona collected the award as the best player of the tournament. Before the game, Maradona strolled to the center of the pitch, where the game ball had been placed, flicked the ball into the air, and started juggling. As he juggled he used all parts of his body: his head, shoulders, thighs, and chest. It was wonderful to watch, and it was easy to see that Maradona had confidence and was going to have an amazing game.

If you observe soccer players, you will notice that most, if not all, of the ones who have good touches are also very good at juggling. Therefore, it is imperative to start on juggling with kids at a very young age.

Do this drill first thing every practice, or as the last thing before any player can leave. Have the players, each with a ball in his hands, drop the ball to their feet, hit it back up waist high, and catch it. They must keep doing this (foot to hand) for thirty to fifty times each practice. Have them do this at a slow pace until they start getting really good and comfortable; then increase the speed at which you want them to do it.

Next, instruct them that as they try to do their fifty kicks, the players should try to kick the ball up two to three times before catching the ball. Again, as they get comfortable (and only as they get comfortable), increase the touches (juggles) to three to five times, and so on, until they can get to about eight to ten juggles in a row without catching the ball. Once they can do eight to ten before catching the ball, they are not allowed to use their hands any more. Now at each practice, the minimum requirement is eight to ten juggles, but challenge the players to do as many as possible.

Many soccer stores sell patches specifically made to commemorate the number of juggles that a player can do. Trying to earn this patch can be motivational for your players. Early on in the learning process, have a bag of patches with the number 10 or 20 on them to award to a player who makes that many juggles in a row.

Remember not to increase the minimum juggles level until they are comfortable with the previous level. It might take all season or even two seasons for some players to advance. It doesn't matter; they must be comfortable first with each level and shouldn't be rushed. Otherwise, you do not accomplish anything other than hurting their confidence.

Complex Drills (Scenarios)

Simple drills are useful for teaching individual skills, but we believe that you must exercise your kids in the execution of scenarios that use multiple skills and put them into game situations. These complex drills help players practice decision making, not just refine positioning and ballhandling skills. Due to the increased complexities of these drills, we will describe each with three sections: the objective of the drill, how to setup for the drill, and directions how to execute the drill.

The five complex drills, or scenarios, are:

1. 3v3/3v2 Counterattack
2. 2v2
3. 3v2 Offense vs. Defense
4. Bread and Butter
5. 4v4 Small-Sided Game

1. 3v3/3v2 Counterattack

Objective: Encourage a quick attack and for your players to spread out as they go downfield. Use this drill when your team is lethargic on the attack or unable to penetrate defenses, even when it has the advantage in numbers of players.

Setup: The playing area required is about half of the soccer field, arranged as shown below.

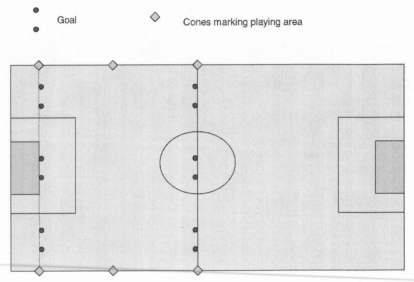

● Goal ◇ Cones marking playing area

You need only half of the field for the 3v3/3v2 counterattack drill.

Directions: Divide the team into two halves with an equal number of play-ers. You need at least twelve players total to do this drill. Start with three players from each team and one ball on the field, plus a couple of balls at each small goal. Each team has to defend its three small goals on its side. We use three goals rather than one to increase the options for the offense, to hone passing and defensive skills, and to permit smaller goals, which makes scoring more dif-ficult. Additionally, using three smaller goals instead of one larger goal allows you to rotate new players in more efficiently.

You need to have one or two balls at each goal, along with the remaining players (who are not playing on the field) on each side evenly spread across the three goals. These other players should stand behind the three goals, just off of the field, waiting to sprint on to the field when needed.

Start the drill by having one team kickoff. The game is played similarly to a real game. If the ball goes out the side of the field, then a kick-in is performed. If it goes out the end line, then the team that gets the ball (the team that did not touch it last) gets to perform a kick-in from where it went out on the end line. While a kick-in is not a set play in a soccer game, it substitutes for a pass from a fixed location.

When a goal is scored, things happen fast, so your players must pay attention. The team that scored the goal does not change. They stay on the field. However, the player who scored must run around the goal that he just scored on three times. The team that was scored on immediately leaves the field and is replaced by three new players—one player from each goal enters the field. The player at the goal that was scored on will start with the ball.

These three new players now mount a counterattack against the two players still on the field, since the third player, the one who scored, has to do three laps around the goal just scored on. Notice that this counterattack starts with the three players spread out. Encourage this counterattack to be fast, smart, and efficient to take advantage of the three to two advantage. If the new offensive team hesitates, then it will give the opponent time to get its third player back, thus negating the temporary advantage.

X   Players on one squad

O   Players on other squad

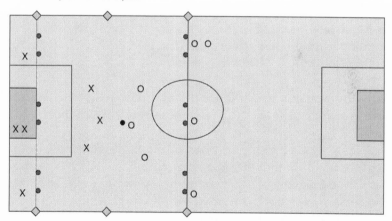

The 3v3/3v2 counterattack demands your team focus on rapid counterattacks and precise passing.

Encourage the defensive team to provide steady *pressure and cover* early on to disrupt the flow of the offense down the field to make time for the third player (the scorer) to get back into play. Steady pressure and cover means to cut off passing lanes while also slightly hurrying the person with the ball, hoping he will make an errant pass or a backpass. Both of these options will provide enough time for the third defensive player to make it back on to the field. Do not double-team the player with the ball; with only two defensive players, if the person with the ball makes the pass, no one will be available to stop the offensive team from scoring.

If the kids are not scoring goals quickly, you may have to announce that one side will switch out on a throw-in or kick-in. Just yell out, "New red team," or something similar. Get your players attuned to these rapid switchovers in squads. This drill is fast paced. So while there are only six players on the field at once, the ones who are not playing must keep alert, since they may have to come on the field at anytime.

2. 2v2

Objective: Ensure that your offensive players are attacking the opponent's goal, that they know how to get open quickly for a pass, and that they take quick, powerful shots. You want to reinforce that they cannot fiddle around with the ball. This drill also encourages your defensive players to mark up quickly on their opponents; since the goals are only twenty yards apart, most players are a threat to shoot at any point in the playing area. Overall, this drill helps to hone your players' offensive and defensive aggressiveness.

You can also consider this drill practice at quickly mounting an offensive attack when your team has the ball in your opponent's 18 yard line.

Setup: This drill is performed on half of the field. Ideally, use one of the actual goals on the field and then set up a second one of the same width. It would be best to drag one of the goals to the halfway line. (Note: If you ever move a goal, make sure that it is secured so that it cannot tip over.) Divide the team into two squads that line up beside their respective goal in two lines, as shown in the figure below. Each team does have a goalkeeper in its goal.

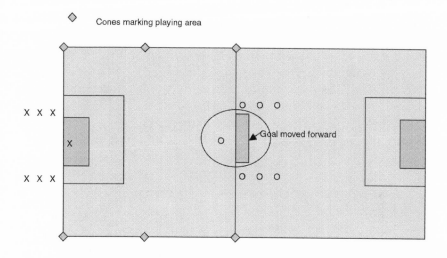

The 2v2 drill helps to reinforce smart, but aggressive, play by playing on a short field (i.e. half the field) and focusing on scoring and preventing scoring quickly.

Directions: Two players from each team start at the middle of the field. Toss the ball into play and instruct both teams to try to score. This 2v2 setup requires each player to make quick, decisive moves to get open quickly. This is a very offensive-minded activity. Run a 2v2 game for one minute or until one squad scores. The two players on the squad that scored stay on the field, while the team that was scored on sprints off the field.

The goalkeeper gives the ball to the new squad. If a squad wins four times in a row, then replace those players with a new squad. Otherwise, the team that scores stays on the field.

If a team attempts a shot and no one from the other team touches the ball before it crosses the endline, the kicking team would normally get a goal kick. However, the kicking team gets to stay while the defending squad must leave the field. We do this to encourage squads to take shots.

This drill does not stop. Continue this scenario for ten to fifteen minutes, or until your players need a break.

3. 3v2 Offense vs. Defense

Objective: Encourage offensive players to use the entire field to spread out the defense by using quick passes and shots when open. The spacing should open up the use of good crosses to the outside forwards, who should look to beat the one defender to the open space. Defensive players should focus on disciplined pressure and cover techniques, where they attack the person with the ball but do not overcommit to the ball handler.

Setup: Divide the team into two squads, offense and defense. The players on the offensive squad are evenly spread across the three offensive stations, as shown in the figure below. The defensive squad is evenly spread across the two defensive stations, plus the goalkeeper position.

◇   Cones marking playing area

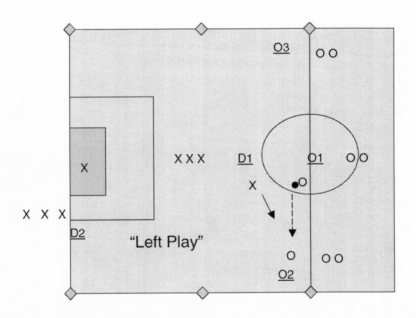

The 3v2 offense vs. defense scenario closely resembles an offensive run from the halfway line.

Directions: The play starts at the first offensive station (O1). There are two variations of this drill: left play and right play. In the left play, the offensive player at O1 passes the ball to the left (to O2) and the defensive player at D1 immediately pursues O2.

As soon as O1 passes the ball to O2 from O1, the second defensive player takes the field from his station, D2. Note that you plan ahead which side a player will play, left or right, so that the D2 station is on the side of the goal to which O1 makes the initial pass. The figure above is for left play; for right play, move the D2 station to the other side of the goal.

After the defense has taken the ball or knocked it out of play, return the ball to station O1. The first person in the line gets ready for the next session.

You may keep the same player at goalkeeper or have a line at goalkeeper as a station D3, if you want more than one player to get practice at goalkeeper.

4. Bread and Butter

Objective: This drill works on crisp passing, soft first touches, spacing, and shooting. How well your team plays inside either 18 yard line is critical because this is the position from which most goals are scored. So this drill is designed to keep your team inside the 18 yard line the whole time. Maintaining the appropriate offensive and defensive intensity during this drill is important, as it will likely determine how your team reacts in this situation during a match.

Setup: The playing area is the 18 yard box on a standard soccer field, with the second goal moved up to the 18 yard line so you have a very short field, as shown in the diagram below. Each goal has a goalkeeper, who stays in the entire drill. Divide your team into three or four squads of four to five players each. All of the players, except the goalkeepers, start by lining up along the 18 yard box.

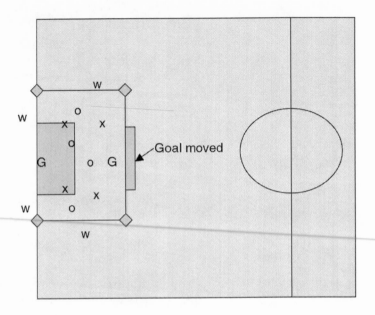

◇ Cones marking playing area

The Bread and Butter drill is played inside the 18 yard line with ten players requiring rapid decision making and precise passing.

Directions: The game starts with two teams on the field evenly spread. In the diagram above, the first two teams playing are the *x*'s and *o*'s, while the *w*'s are the third squad. Start the game by throwing the ball up at midfield. The two teams play a 4v4 or 5v5 game in this small region. Throw-ins are taken the same as during a regular game; however, goal kicks and corner kicks are also taken as throw-ins by the appropriate squad.

This game never stops. Each session is played to two goals or two minutes, whichever occurs first. When a team scores for the first time, the goalkeeper takes the ball and passes it to his teammates, who try to counterattack.

When a team scores for the second time, the defensive team sprints off the field and is immediately replaced by the next squad (or other squad, depending on how many squads you have). The squad that scored stays on the field as long as they keep winning the sessions. When a squad scores, the goalkeeper for the winning side immediately kicks a ball on the field to start the new squad from its goal. They do not wait for the defending squad to get situated.

For this reason, players on the squad waiting to come on to the field should space themselves out around the perimeter of the playing area in order to make a run at the opponent's goal. If all of the players from an oncoming squad are in one place, then they have to run a good distance to get spread out; whereas if they are situated all around the playing area, they can quickly cover the entire area.

Run this drill for thirty minutes, keeping track of the number of sessions each team wins.

5. 4v4 Small-Sided Game

Objective: 4v4 small-sided games are the best drill for developing players, since they provide the minimum number of players to cover all principles of soccer play.

Setup: This game is played on half of the soccer field turned sideways, as shown in the diagram below. The goals are marked by cones on opposite side-lines. There are no goalkeepers.

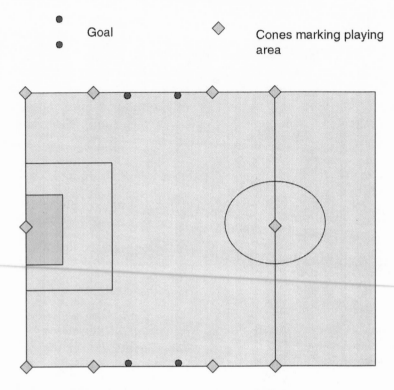

The 4v4 small-sided scrimmage is an important drill since it creates numerous opportunities for the players to engage in game-like situations.

Directions: This is simply a scrimmage, but several configurations of the four players should be used, reinforced, and commented on often. These configurations will all be relevant for use in 6v6, 7v7, 8v8, and even 11v11 games.

Each of the three primary configurations is shown below, along with the primary purpose of each. The #1 position on each is considered the target, or focus, of the configuration. The two supporting players (#2 and #3) provide width to the formation, while the last player (#4) provides depth.

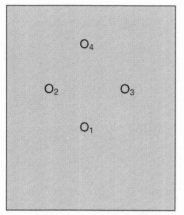
Offensive Positioning

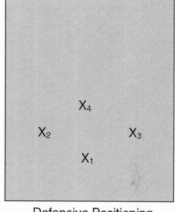
Defensive Positioning

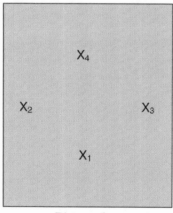
Diamond

The diamond shape is basically a couple of connected triangles with the same concept of supporting one's teammate, as discussed in the triangle drill. On offense, you have every possible combination of pass and play without anybody being left out. Similarly, on defense, the diamond provides all of the potential requirements for practicing pressure and cover sequences with each player having a specific task, but with no two players having the same task.

Donahue is demonstrating a good defensive stance by bending his knees, being on his toes, and looking at the ball. He is close enough to slow down his opponent's progress, but not so close that the ball handler can easily passed him.

Play a 4v4 game when the number of players in your practice allows you to break up the team into squads of four. It is often useful to play one 4v4 game while taking four other players aside to work on some fundamental skill, such as trapping, heading, or the foot strike. In this way, you break up the team into several squads and keep them busy all practice long, doing the most efficient drills possible.

Instructional Scrimmaging

Beyond drills and scenarios, it is essential to have your players spend as much time as possible actually playing practice games (scrimmages) and games. The ultimate goal when coaching a good youth soccer player is grooming someone who makes good, quick decisions. This is best taught by putting players into the situation where a decision is required again and again.

Normally, in scrimmages you want to have the same-sided games as you will have in your official games so that the same spacing and positions are all reinforced. If you do not have enough players to have two full sides, you can put some coaches, parents, and/or siblings out on the field. However, you need to make sure that older siblings and parents are careful not to play so hard as to hurt one of your players, but also not so easy that they are not posing a realistic challenge.

Having coaches intermingled with your players also provides the opportunity for several people to discretely give advice. For instance, you might have a parent play one of your two fullbacks. That parent/coach can advise the other fullback on how he should rotate and talk to the other fullback, for example.

You should be on the field at the beginning of the scrimmage. Blow your whistle often and stop play to discuss positioning, decision making, and confidence. Try hard to catch your kids doing things right. Do not blow the whistle only when something bad happens. It is usually a good idea to stop the first half of any instructional scrimmage with frequent whistles and instruction. During the second half, reduce the interruptions to see if your players correct their mistakes, such as poor spacing between players, on their own.

Scrimmages are just like drills. They are a results-driven exercise, so do not overemphasizing winning. We suggest that you never keep track of goals during scrimmages. Rather, select some other skill that you want them to improve and give points for that. We often give points for any of the following accomplishments, depending on the age and skill level of the team:

- any passes
- crossing passes
- tackles,
- trapping the ball in the air
- using the left foot for a shot (even if it does not go in)
- headers

Positions and Positioning

Overall, you want to keep the middle of the field strong. Forcing the other team to the outside moves them away from your goal. However, while this sounds simple, it is the result of years of working on positioning.

Do not be satisfied with random motion on the field. Young players, even at the peewee level, can function great as a team as long as you provide lessons that are simple and reinforced with visual teaching aids. Youth players can do more than you expect, but you must use handouts and provide simple rules to follow.

A common mistake for the highly athletic but uncoached soccer player is to run after the ball rather than run to a point on the field that best prevents the forward motion of the ball. We have said hundreds of times to the young players to run in straight lines.

The smallest and slowest kid on your team can be the best at positioning. This ability provides confidence for the weaker player because he has something to excel in on the field. We have found that the intelligence to be in the right place makes up for lots of foot speed and ballhandling skills. Good positioning skills also provide the novice player with the versatility to play multiple positions. This is important because you may not really know the best place for a child to play right away. Just because a player is fast does not mean that he should be a forward or midfielder. Similarly, just because he is big and tough does not mean that he should be a fullback.

The most important aspect of positioning is that being in the right place is the best way to help one's team. We have talked about teaching your players to trust their teammates by staying in their position and doing their job. There is no need to overplay to help out a teammate when it will just turn the game into magnet ball.

The table below shows how the discussion of positioning will evolve over the years of youth soccer. For peewee players, have them consider only the ball and the goal as cues as to where they should be playing. In the middle years, you must add the sidelines and other members of the team to the positioning process. The tween player must also learn to react to the positioning of his opponents.

	Relative To				
	Ball	Goal	Sidelines	Your Team	Opposing Team
Peewee	X	X			
Middle Years	X	X	X	X	
Tween Years	X	X	X	X	X

The rubric for positioning is a valuable way to help your players evolve naturally over the years.

Start using proper terms for positions as early as possible to get the children to do the same. The typical positions are listed below:

The *goalkeeper* plays in your goal and is allowed to use her hands when inside the 18 yard line.

The *sweeper* plays closest to the goalkeeper and is defensive minded. This position is often called a *center fullback*.

Fullbacks play close to the goalkeeper and are defensive minded.

Midfielders are responsible for transitioning the ball down the field and preventing the opponent from transitioning the ball into your end of the field.

Halfbacks and *forwards* play closer to the opponent's goal and are primarily offensive-minded. Outside halfbacks and forwards are often called *wings*.

A *striker* is purely offensive minded. He plays closest to the opponent's goal, and his job is to score goals. This position is often called a *center forward*.

Peewee (4v4)

There are only three things that you should say at this level:

1. Keep your eyes on the ball.
2. Go to the imaginary line on defense and away from the imaginary line on offense.
3. Have fun.

There are no goalkeepers in the 4v4 game, but you will routinely have one player who is primarily defensive (a fullback). The three other players are spread out across the field and are halfbacks. Many teams do not call their players anything at this age, but starting to use soccer terminology now makes the kids feel cool and eliminates relearning moments later.

The diagram below shows how your players should be arranged at the kickoff relative to your goal.

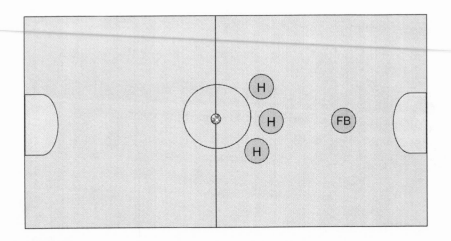

In peewee soccer there are four field players: three halfbacks, plus one player with the defensive responsibility similar to a fullback's.

Peewee soccer is usually marked by the chaotic crowd around wherever the ball is. If the child is not picking flowers or watching the dog on the sidelines, then he is running after the ball in a swarm.

Impress upon your players that you know (and they do too) where the other team is going. They are trying to head toward your goal! Remind your players not to chase the ball. Instead, they should go to where the person with the ball is probably going and then attack the ball. Where the other team is going with the ball is the imaginary line we discussed earlier in the rope drill. This critical skill will be useful in later years.

When your team has the ball in your opponent's end of the field, the full-back does not stand back by his own goal. The fullback should move up as far as the halfway line and think of himself as the last person who can stop the opponents from scoring a goal. The fullback should stay on that imaginary line between the ball and his goal even when the ball is way down the field. This way, he likely will slow down or at least be in the best position to challenge the oncoming player. Fullbacks will use this alignment all the way through the middle years, so this is a good foundation.

When playing offense, your players without the ball should stay away from the imaginary line. This creates space for their teammate with the ball, which gives that player the best chance to score or to pass the ball to a teammate. The diagram below shows this action.

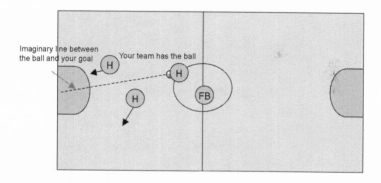

If you can get your players to think about making space on offense, your team will have some fun out on the field and you will have laid a great foundation for the middle years.

When your team is playing defense, the peewee alignment is based on the rope drill, as shown below. On defense, the fullback maintains a closer prox-imity to your goal but still responds to the imaginary line and works with the halfbacks to provide resistance along the shortest distance to the goal.

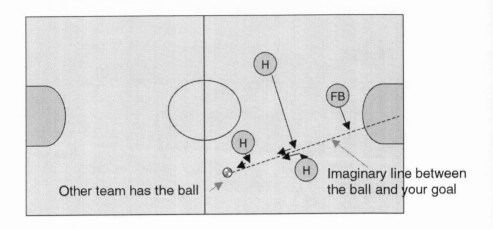

You have seen this figure before, but it is important and thus worth repeating, since learning the angles and movement without the ball is critical for youth soccer.

Middle Years (6v6)

As stated earlier, positioning for the middle years is determined relative to not only the ball and the goal, but also the sidelines and one's teammates. The primary issue for this stage is for the players to understand their position's responsibility on the field.

Whereas in the peewee years we stress watching the ball and going to the imaginary line, in the middle years we focus on spacing and keeping in one's lanes. This is possible to get straight only through the use of visual aids, hand-outs, and quizzes, which reinforces that soccer is a thinking game. It is critical to reinforce the importance of making and denying space on offense and defense, respectively, since any team with a solid offense and defense will fare quite well. It is better at this stage to have a balanced team with no superstars.

In addition, we have selected arrangements that keep the middle strong and give everyone a simple decision to make. Once each player has a simple decision to make, then everyone has more confidence.

The diagram below shows the layout for the 6v6 formation. Typically, two fullbacks stand side by side. However, that is better for more advanced players. For this age group, stacking the fullbacks, one in front of the other, is more effective. We call the one closer to midfield the attacking fullback. This configuration helps focus the players on simple and effective decision making while also keeping the middle strong.

In fact, lining up the fullback and attacking fullback along the line between the ball and your goal is just like the peewees getting to the imaginary line. The idea is to ensure that the defenders are in the perfect position to defend their goal from the ball.

This arrangement is both effective and irregular (in comparison to soccer norms). It is effective since the job of the fullbacks is very clear now. The attacking fullback heads straight to the person with the ball to disrupt that player's movement down the field. It is irregular because most soccer books put the fullbacks next to each other. In that arrangement, the fullbacks have to decide who will go after the ball as it heads into their end of the field. But that is especially difficult when the ball is coming down the middle of the field.

We came up with this alternate approach since we could not provide any clear guidance to our players on how to decide which fullback should go after the oncoming ball first, so we just shifted one fullback up.

In the 6v6 formation, note the strength down the middle. This arrangement should force the other team to the outside, where it is more difficult to score.

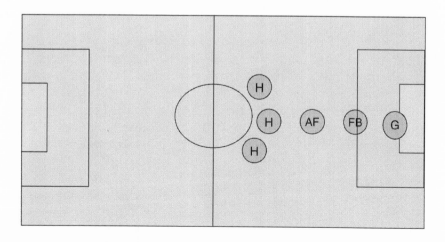

In the 6v6 formation, the middle is kept strong.

We will now describe each position in the 6v6 formation in detail. These descriptions are critical since they start to tie together many of the skills and tactics discussed previously in this book.

Goalkeeper. The goalkeeper is both a glamorous and nerve-racking, position for the youth soccer player. He can be the big hero or feel as if he let the other team score. It is an important life lesson to start early in the 5v5 or 6v6 formations that any goal scored by your team is the result of all of the players on the field, and not just the last person to touch it before it goes into the goal. Girls resonate with this sentiment much more than boys at this age.

Similarly, when the other team scores a goal against your team, you must emphasize that everyone on the team shares the responsibility of stopping a goal. The goalkeeper depends on all of her teammates to prevent the other team from getting close enough to take easy shots. Girls are especially susceptible to erosion of their confidence when goals go rolling in.

Most youth soccer leagues require that you play different kids as goalkeeper for each half of the game. The leagues do not want anyone solely used as a goalkeeper so early in their careers. This keeps one child from being in the goal all of the time if your defense is not so good. In addition, this helps all the players understand that defense is a real team effort; it is not up to the goalkeeper alone. You will see a real change in the intensity of a fullback, for instance, after playing half of a game as goalkeeper.

Many books and programs focus on goalkeeper training. We will concentrate only on the basics. As kids get to around ten or eleven years old, a few of them will start to focus on being a goalkeeper exclusively. You will not be able to keep up with their training, but pay attention to their efforts. It is amazing how much children can learn when challenged and coached by quality personnel. Goalkeeper is the first position where you will see this special focus, but in later years players go to special goal-scoring camps and defensive-training sessions.

In the meantime, you can offer three main coaching tips for goalkeepers: move your feet and use your hands, learn the angles, and talk to your teammates.

Many first-time goalkeepers want to dive for the ball, but you want to encourage them to get as much of their body in front of the ball as possible and stay on their feet. If you can get your goalkeeper to get his body in front of the ball, then you are way ahead of everybody else. The goalkeeper should move his feet to get between the ball and the goal, so if the ball slips through his hands, it will hit his shins, legs, or chest.

Your goalkeeper need not be afraid to get his hands up and on the ball. There is no shortage of suggestions for advanced goalkeeping with regard to how he holds his hands relative to the shot location. But the first threshold is to get a young player who is not afraid of the ball and who can actually catch the ball.

Angles are very important. The beginner goalkeeper is likely to want to stay right in front of the goal. However, the farther back the goalkeeper stays, the easier he is making it for the person shooting on the goal, especially in youth soccer. This is true for two reasons. First, at this age the goalkeeper is often passive. However, being aggressive and pressing the other team to make a decision, rather than waiting for them to take a shot, puts the goalkeeper in charge. It is much better to make a decision, act, and make the other team react, than it is to wait for the other team to do something and then, hopefully, respond well to the challenge. Take charge!

Second, geometry is the goalkeeper's friend when he comes out of the goal. In the figure below, you can see in the upper pane that the goalkeeper blocks out only so much of the goal relative to the shooter (player X) when the goalkeeper is right on the goal line. Clearly, the goalkeeper can react to the shot and move to his right or left to block it. However, if the goalkeeper comes out of the goal, then he blocks out more of the goal than before, effectively taking it away from the shooter.

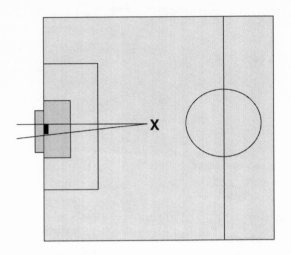

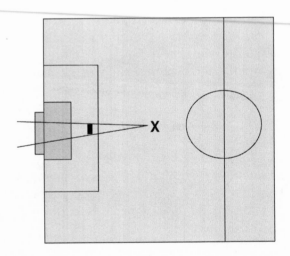

Coming out of the goal helps the goalkeeper cover more of the goal, but he must be aware of other opponents who might be available for a pass from the opponent approaching the goal.

As the goalkeeper comes out of the goal to challenge the shooter and take away the shooting angles, he must consider several factors to determine how far out to come: strength of the person shooting, other opponents nearby available for a pass, and any defensive support from their own team.

Darren McKnight, PhD and Radovan Pletka

The goalkeeper has the best view of the field and as such needs to have the confidence to assist the rest of the team in positioning themselves against their opponents. The goalkeeper should not tell everybody on his team how to play their position, but he can provide some insights about how the other team is advancing and also how vulnerable he feels. For example, the goalkeeper may yell out, "Who has got number seven? He's wide open!" or, "Help me on the right side!"

Goalkeepers can use their hands inside the 18 yard line, but do not forget that he may dribble the ball anywhere on the field, like anyone else. It might be effective for the goalkeeper to roll the ball on the ground outside of the 18 yard line, then step into a big kick.

Whenever the ball is within the 18 yard line, your players must be right on it. They cannot let the other team dribble around near their goal.

Fullback. All the players in the 6v6 formation are shown below, with the dashed area representing where the fullback (F) is likely to play.

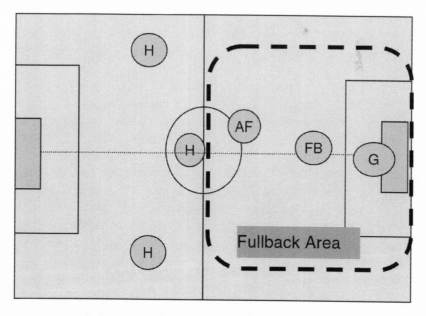

The fullback does not have to cover a lot of ground, but his responsibility is to be the last line of defense for your team. Fullback is an important position that requires sound decision-making skills.

The fullback is primarily defensive. He will not normally cross over the half-way line or ever go all the way into the corners of his own end of the field. There is usually no need to follow teams all the way into the corners at this age, since the other team cannot score from the corner. The halfback, or attacking fullback, should challenge the ball in the corner. The fullback should always stay about midway between the ball and his own goal in a straight line.

The fullback should not run away from the ball (backwards) in the open field. If the other team has made it past the attacking fullback, then the fullback must tackle the opponent decisively. The attacking fullback and/or the weak-side (the side of the field without the ball) halfback will be there to help the fullback. As a matter of fact, if the ball is dribbled right at your fullback, then he knows that the attacking fullback has been beaten. The attacking fullback will be running straight toward his own goal to fill in behind the fullback. This is a defensive rotation and will be shown with the attacking fullback position below.

Teach fullbacks early on that they are not a second goalkeeper. They should stay away from the goal (except when the other team is doing a corner kick). This becomes even more important in the later years when your opponent can strike the ball better. They must play the ball and then other players (pressure the ball) but not drop back into the goalkeeper's area unless an opponent is there.

For everyone, but especially fullbacks, your players should focus on marking up. This means equalizing the opponent within their own 18 yard line by getting hip on hip while staying between them and their own goal. Your players must make sure that they do not let the other team have any easy opportunities inside their own 18 yard line. Sticking to any opponent must become a natural move for your players near their own goal. For players in the middle years, this almost always means to react to opponents within their 18 yard line, whereas when your team reaches the tween years, it may be necessary to mark up on players on your half of the field (depending on the strength of their legs).

Marking up is also not always a hip on hip. In the middle years, we often use this term to focus on making the defense man on man. However, in the tween years, players have a tendency to mark up with more space between them and their opponent, but with the knowledge and anticipation that they know how to get to the player they are covering very quickly. As opponents get faster, it is critical to play a little farther off in order to be less susceptible to fakes and jukes. As the opponents get faster, so will your players, so you need to adjust accordingly.

Attacking fullback. The playing area for the attacking fullback (A) is shown below.

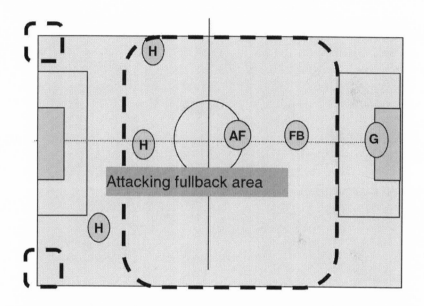

We came up with the idea for the attacking fullback in the middle years to help with the defensive decision-making process.

The attacking fullback plays up farther than the fullback. His primary job is to keep the ball out of his end of the field. The attacking fullback is the first person to attack the ball as it comes into his half of the field. Once he attacking fullback takes the ball, he tries to transition the ball into the opponent's end of the field either by dribbling or passing (he should never pass the ball if no one is pressuring him). The attacking fullback normally will transition the ball to a halfback at or near the halfway line.

We have found it useful to assign a single person on the field to take corner kicks. For the 6v6 formation, we suggest that the attacking fullback do this. This leaves all of the halfbacks available for attacking the opponent's goal from the corner kick. However, the attacking fullback must hustle back into position around the middle of the field once he has made the kick. In addition, the attacking fullback will always take the throw-ins.

As you can see, the attacking fullback is a key player in the 6v6. This player should be strong and not afraid of oncoming players.

Halfbacks. The right halfback stays on the right side and dribbles the ball down the field, or passes it to the middle or all the way to the other side of the field. When the ball goes to the other side of the field, the halfback should not go past the center of the field, as shown in the diagram below. This type of discipline is tough for young kids because they have been told that the harder they run after the ball, the better they are. However, this is where you start teaching them to play as a team and trust their teammates.

This is true for all positions, but it is especially important for halfbacks in the 6v6 formation, since they must keep their lanes to ensure that the other team cannot progress down the field easily and so that the offense has more potential scoring opportunities.

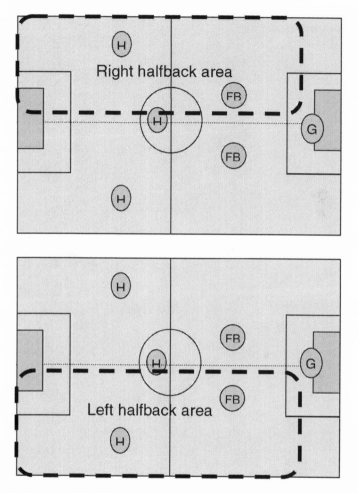

In short-sided games, the halfbacks are a combination of the midfielders (who transition from defense to offense) and forwards (who kick the ball into the goal).

When halfbacks close in on the opponent's goal, they should shoot for the far post. This means the side of the goal farthest from them. This is the best shot to take for several reasons. At this age, the goalkeeper will almost always overplay to the side of the ball. In addition, if the halfback misses it to the outside, then the ball might go toward another teammate, thus providing another opportunity to score. If they miss the shot to the inside, then the ball will at least go toward the goal, where it may bounce off of the goalkeeper, providing another opportunity for your team.

If a player shoots for the goalpost nearest to the ball, it may travel uselessly out of bounds or straight to the goalkeeper. Since the shooter is heading downfield, the ball will naturally go straight down the field; so shooting it at the far post will make it more likely that the ball will fade into the goal. If the halfback shoots it to the near post, the natural fade will pull the ball uselessly out of bounds and give your opponent a goal kick.

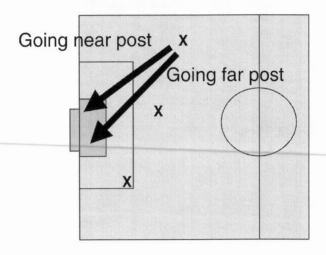

When a shooter goes far post versus near post, many more good outcomes can occur.

The center halfback is another versatile position in the 6v6 formation. This person must run the most and be able to pass, defend, and shoot.

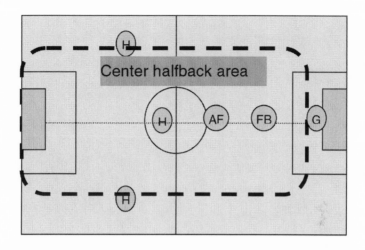

The center halfback covers a lot of ground and is always battling in the middle of the field.

The center halfback must stay near the middle of the field and then pass back to the outside halfbacks, if not taking a shot himself. Defensively, the center halfback must ensure that the other team does not have a clear shot down the middle of the field. He should force the play to the outside or steal the ball away.

Overall play. The general flow of the ball from your own goal, down the field, and then toward your opponent's goal is out, down, and in.

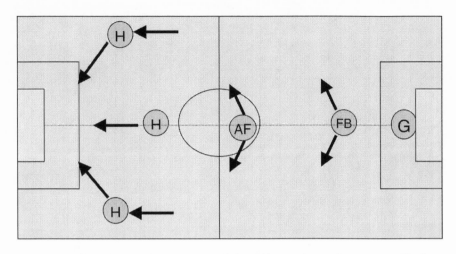

The general flow of the ball from your goal should be out (away from your goal), down (down the field), and in (toward your opponent's goal).

When the ball is near your goal, the intent is to move the ball to the outside, away from your goal. In later years, you might encourage your players to pass it back across in front of your goal, but not until they have mastered the ability to make quick, accurate passes. The intent of getting the ball *out* is to get it both away from your goal and away from the bulk of the players in the hope of making it down the field more quickly.

It also is important to get the ball into your opponent's end of the field. Once the fullback passes the ball to the outside, then your players need to get it down the field. More players are usually near the center of the field than near the sidelines, so take advantage of this and get the ball into your opponent's end of the field.

Once the ball is in your opponent's end, get the ball into the middle of the field, where your players are and the goal is. You do not want to run the ball all the way into the corner of the opponent's end of the field, so try to pass to the middle and/or shoot. Anytime that you can get the ball heading toward the opponent's goal, good things are likely to happen for your team. Either they will get the ball to another player, or the ball might go into the goal. One thing is for sure: if they do not have a plan, the ball will not likely end up in the opponent's goal.

Your players must be able to trust their teammates to play their own positions. Stress the importance of passing the ball to the open space; their teammates will get there. If no one is open, then your player should pass the ball to the open space toward the other goal. If nothing else, the ball will roll for a while and give your players a chance to get to it.

Emphasize that all players play both offense and defense. As we just reviewed the positions, it should have been obvious that while fullbacks are primarily defensive and halfbacks are primarily offensive, all players have some responsibilities for both offense and defense. Any goal cored is the result of all of the players on the team doing their job, not just the last player to touch the ball before it goes into the net.

Throw-ins. Throw-ins are interesting plays in youth soccer. It is the one time that the players, other than the goalkeeper, can use their hands, and at these young ages your players will be much more accurate with their hands than with their feet.

However, the throw-in play for the middle years really depends upon the type of players that you have. If you have a big kid who can throw the ball twenty to thirty yards reliably, it is almost always best to have that player heave the ball down the field. Most of your players will not have that strong of a throw-in, so you need to set up the team for the real intent of a throw-in: to maintain possession with an opportunity to advance it down the field. A throw-in play uses the advice you have read often so far: spread out, make good decisions, and attack the ball.

When your team has the throw-in, you must make three important decisions.

First, who is going to throw the ball in? This is critical because a throw-in becomes more effective if it is executed quickly, before the other team can set up a strong defense. The person throwing in the ball should be fairly close to where the ball went out. More important, his teammates need to arrange themselves relative to the thrower in order to maximize the probability of maintaining possession of the ball. Generally, throw-ins will be taken by the player positioned on that side of the field. Therefore, in your defensive end, the attacking fullback (or same-side fullback for 8v8) will take throw-ins, while in your offensive end, the strongside halfback (or equivalent) will perform the throw-in.

Second, where will the thrower throw the ball? The teammates of the one throwing in the ball should be arranged with a purpose in mind. It is important to have a plan, especially for the middle years (normally there are no throw-ins for peewee soccer), because set plays provide a framework for how your team reacts during a throw-in. Is the opponent aggressive on the players near the sideline or focused on preventing any throw-ins toward their goal? Whatever the other team does, your players must respond and make good decisions. In the middle years you usually want throw-ins going away from your goal because if the ball is mishandled, it is better for the turnover to occur as far away from your goal as possible.

In the tween years, however, your team's confidence and skill level will increase, so it is much more likely that your players will make throw-ins back toward your goal. This dimension of the game comes into play about the same time that your players start to use and benefit from backpasses.

Third, does the receiving player have a plan? For tweens, it is critical that the receiving player, as well as the person throwing the ball in, has a plan. When receiving a throw-in, your players must be able to sense where their opponents are in order to make the right first move with the ball. A safe technique is to have the receiving player immediately pass it back to the person who just threw in the ball, because he is normally left uncovered. In addition, the thrower has a good perspective on where players are located around the field, especially since no one lurking behind him.

When your team is defending a throw-in, you must determine what your team's intentions are. Do you want to pressure the team to try to force a turn-over, or just prevent them from advancing down the field toward your goal? In a close game in which your team trails, it might be prudent to aggressively try to intercept a throw-in. But if you are winning, you might want to play it safe and ensure that the opponent does not advance the ball toward your goal.

No matter which approach your team takes, the first priority is to arrange the players relative to the other team while anticipating the opponent's potential movement. A typical risk-return equation plays out multiple times throughout the course of a match during throw-ins: do you play aggressively, looking to win possession of the ball back, at the risk of letting the other team advance toward your goal?

To reiterate, how your team plays a throw-in largely depends upon the situation within the game but also on the general skill level and speed of the other team relative to your players.

Corner kick play. We covered corner kicks in chapter four. For the 6v6 formation, we suggest bringing up the attacking fullback to perform the corner kick. This player needs to try hard to get the ball into the air so that the opponent cannot easily intercept it. After the kick, the attacking fullback needs to hustle back toward the halfway line.

Defensive rotation. When the ball is dribbled into your end of the field, normally the attacking fullback is the first person to contest the other team. As long as this player maintains that line between the ball and his own goal, he will attack the ball moving directly away from his own goal.

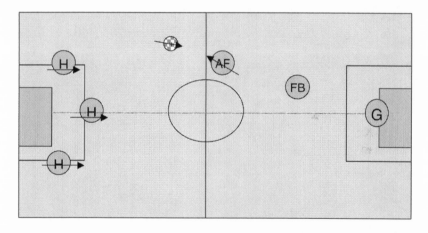

The attacking fullback is the first player to challenge an oncoming opponent as that opponent approaches the attacking fullback's goal, while the fullback remains in a line between the attacking fullback and his own goal.

Fullbacks should not be within ten feet of each other normally. They want to be far enough away from each other to take up as much space as possible while still being close enough that they can support each other (through pressure and cover).

When the other team starts to bring the ball down toward your defenders and your halfbacks have not caught up to the ball yet, the attacking fullback needs to commit to the ball and the fullback must go halfway between the attacking fullback and his goal. This way, if an opponent is going to make it to the goal, that player will have to beat both fullbacks.

If the attacking fullback is beaten, then the fullback attacks the ball while the attacking fullback loops back between the ball and the goal. He does not try to recover the ball.

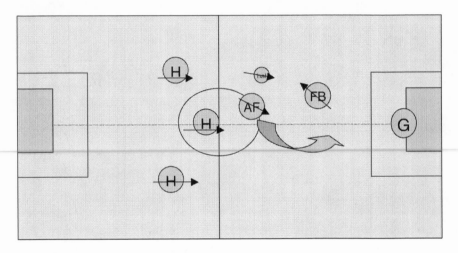

Once the attacking fullback is beaten, he races back (rotates) behind the fullback in a line between the ball and his own goal.

Tweens (8v8)

At the tween level, formations increase to 8v8, the last tier before players move up to the full 11v11, which officially signals the end of youth soccer. As you would expect, at this level you have many effective combinations in which to lay out your eight players. We will explain the two basic formations most often used and how you can switch back and forth with these formations.

The 2-3-2 formation (two fullbacks, three midfielders, two forwards, along with one goalkeeper) provides the most balanced approach to the game: offense, transition, and defense. The figure below shows how the players are positioned.

We do not show the exact coverage for each player (as we did for the 6v6 formation) because by this age the players have become very good about keeping in their lanes and staying in their position. In addition, players will not only react to the field and their teammates, but also to the other team, which requires you to give them more flexibility. It is highly likely that two neighboring players, such as a center midfielder and a right midfielder, might cross to better exploit the positioning of the opponent.

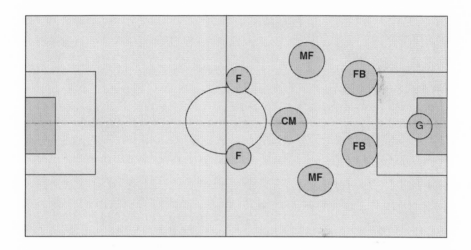

The fullbacks are lined up side to side in the 8v8 formation. The better passing and speed of this age group requires more breadth to the defense.

Player responsibilities. The two forwards (F) are primarily offensive and must stay wide on offense to keep the field open for the center midfielder (CM). The center midfielder must move the ball up the field and make good passes upfield to the forwards. The center midfielder (usually called the center middie) is a critical player in this formation. The center middie must be strong down the middle of the field offensively (does not get pushed out to the side) and defensively (forces the initial attack by the other team to the outside). When the center middie is forced to the outside, the sidelines act as another opponent, since if the ball goes out of bounds the opponent loses the ball.

The outside midfielders (MF), along with the center middie, are responsible for transitioning the ball from their end of the field to their opponent's end and for preventing the other team from advancing down to their end of the field. Normally, the ball does not come straight down the field, so there is the side of the field where the ball is (the strongside) and the side where the ball is not (the weakside). As before, the primary motion of the ball when one of your fullbacks stops the opponent's offensive attack is to clear the ball to the outside (by the fullbacks), transition it down the field (by the outside midfielders), and turn the ball toward the goal (by the forwards). Sometimes the outside midfielders carry the ball down the sidelines or pass to the center middie or the strongside forward.

Defensive rotation. The weakside outside midfielder is crucial on defense. The primary job of the fullbacks (FB) is to defend their goal from an offensive attack by the other team. As the ball approaches, the closest fullback will quickly and decisively attack the ball and try to win it. The other fullback will rotate to between his goal and the ball to prepare for passes made by the attacking player with the ball or to assist if that offensive player beats his fullback. The weakside outside midfielder then must provide weakside defensive help by sliding into the weakside fullback position. This is an extension of the defensive rotation used in the 6v6 game because it involves three players rather than two.

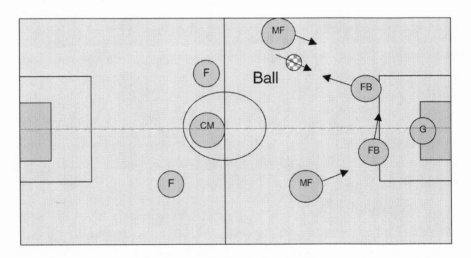

The defensive rotation for the 8v8 formation is similar to the 6v6 defensive rotation.

Note how the strongside outside midfielder is not running toward the opponent with the ball but rather to the open space to the left of the opponent with the ball. In essence, the strongside midfielder is denying space from his opponent. The fullback attacking from the front has the best angle. Your team does not need to double-team anybody this far away from the goal. Instead, they need to attack the ball and stay spread out to intercept the pass.

Set plays. Throw-ins are done in your half of the field by the fullbacks and in the opponent's half of the field by the outside midfielders. Either your goalkeeper or one of the fullbacks can perform goal kicks. At this level, the goalkeeper usually is advanced enough to do the goal kicks. Whoever does the goal kicks needs to be able to get the ball over the opponents' heads and/or to one of his teammates. With a reliable goalkeeper performing goal kicks, there is no need to keep the fullbacks back in the 18 yard line, which helps to transition the ball downfield more reliably.

For corner kicks, select the player from the two forwards and the center middie with the best corner kick. Or, use one of the outside midfielders to do the corner kick to keep the maximum offensive pressure on the other team during this play.

New Concerns for 8v8. Once your team has advanced to the 8v8 formation, the players are stronger and faster. Therefore, the basics we emphasized previously become even more important. Your players should:

• Keep between their opponent and their goal on defense.
• Communicate with their teammates, letting them know what they are doing next and using their names.
• Attack the ball. They should not run backwards and wait to see what the other team is going to do. Instead, they should make the other team react to them.

However, due to the advancing capabilities of older players, there are a few more aspects of the game to deal with. Every player at this level is considered a threat to score if he can get a clean look at the ball within your 18 yard line. As a result, a common cry for this age group must be to mark up in the 18 yard line. This means that if any player from the other team is inside of your 18 yard line, then one of your players should be right next to him. Your player must put his hip on his opponent's hip. In addition to being hip on hip, your player should get between the opponent and his own goal so that he can see the player and, even if the opponent gets the ball, can immediately challenge the opponent for the ball.

As stated, marking up is slightly different for faster, more talented teams. Your players do not want to be right up against their opponents, since they might be able to evade your players quickly. In this case, it is better to position your defensive player so that he is near the opponent, but far enough away to easily react to quick movements. As the ball gets closer to the player your defender is covering, the closer your player will need to be to that opponent. Remind your team that you still know where the other team is heading—toward your goal. Therefore, when marking up, they need to favor their own goal.

Backpass. By the time your team reaches the tween years, the days of pressing down the field and scoring in an all-out rush at the goal are largely over. The offense must have some finesse, using backpasses and changing the field to create some openings in the defense. A backpass is when a player passes back toward his own goal in order for his team to keep possession. This can occur at either end of the field. At the offensive end, a backpass is done to keep the ball from the other team until your team has a better opportunity to advance the ball or shoot. The diagram below shows the typical layout of a backpass in the offensive end of the field. This depicts a backpass from the left side midfielder to the left forward, back to the center middie.

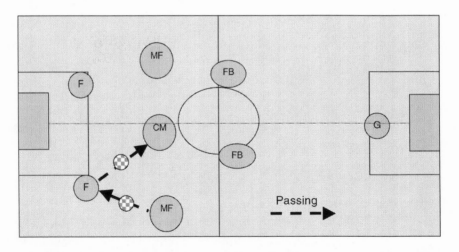

Backpasses help your team maintain possession of the ball while waiting for a clear opening for a scoring opportunity.

Changing the field. The other tactic that a team in the tween years must perfect is changing the field. Changing the field is exactly what it sounds like—you change the side of the field that the ball is on. This takes a few more people and a little more time, but is essentially used for the same reason as a backpass: to maintain possession while your team creates a better opportunity to advance the ball.

Changing the field prevents an opponent from overplaying the ball (putting more players on the strongside of the field). When an opponent overplays your team, your players on the weakside should be wide open. As a result, your players must try to change fields quickly to give their teammates a chance to score.

The diagram below shows one way in which a team may change the field. However, if your team has strong passing skills, they could try to go straight from one outside midfielder directly to the forward on the other side.

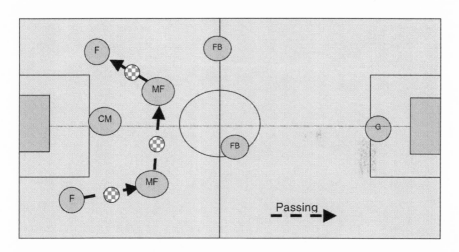

Changing the field is most effective when executed quickly to take advantage of the location of the opponent's players.

Changing to 3-1-3. Sometimes the 2-3-2 formation may not work for your team. Another formation that creates a slightly different style of play is the 3-1-3. The 3-1-3 is stronger up the middle, the tactic used in the peewee and middle years. In addition, the three fullbacks provide for more defensive support. This formation does, however, make the transition of the ball slightly more difficult because it assigns fewer players with the responsibility of transition. Your team also will be susceptible to passes and changing of the field in the middle of the field, providing the other team more opportunities to get the ball into your end of the field.

The diagram below shows how you can switch into a 3-1-3 from a 2-3-2. Decide which formation is best for your team overall, depending upon your players and the types of teams that you play. However, you should teach your team how to transition into the other formation, since it might be useful to do so temporarily during a game or for certain games within a tournament.

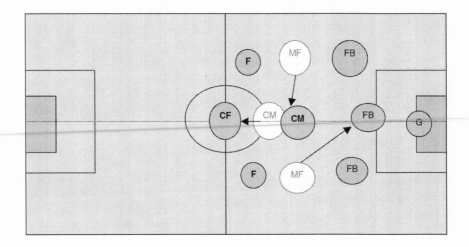

The 3-1-3 formation is stronger down the middle but makes transitioning the ball more difficult.

Three players are directly affected by this change in formation: the center middie shifts up to a center forward, the right midfielder shifts to the center middie, and the left midfielder becomes the center fullback. Your team can do this shift a variety of ways. However, since the center middie and the two forwards work together very closely in the 2-3-2, it is best to move the center middie up between the two forwards. In turn, slide one of the outside midfielders into the new center middie position. The other outside midfielder becomes the center fullback. You may want to adjust your players in these new positions to take advantage of your strongest players. The center fullback is normally the fastest, strongest defender, while the new center middie must be fast and have great enthusiasm for attacking the ball.

A concern with the 3-1-3 is that your "lines" (the two lines of three players) do not actually play in a line. Note how in the diagram above how the line of forwards and the line of fullbacks are slightly staggered; usually the center player is offset by the outside players. This is a much stronger arrangement, creating triangles for optimum passing lanes and providing better angles to prevent the other team from advancing down the field easily.

Back to basics. Sometimes during the course of a season, you must review essentials that your team needs to apply to keep the level of play high. Below is an example review you can use during a tournament or before a game for 8v8.

Back to Basics

• Inside our 18 yard line

> *Ball to the outside*: Goalkeeper punts or throws to the outside midfielder to transition down the field. Goal kicks go to the outside. If the ball is inside our 18 yard line, get it out immediately. If you put a body over the ball, then we can control it. Do not poke at it; run through the ball.

• Between the 18 yard lines

> *Play your position*: Outside midfielders *must* form a triangle with the center middie and forward. You must be available for backpasses and to prevent the fast break. Do not take the ball from a teammate. Forwards must stay on their side of the field so that they can receive crosses and tap in far post shots that go wide.

• In their 18 yard line

> *Shoot (quick and hard)*: Follow everyone's shots. Shoot to the far post and shoot away from the goalkeeper. Do not run around the ball to get to your right foot. Shoot it! Get it out now!

• Overall Issues

> *Communications*: On the field, talk to each other more. On the sideline, we will be talking less. If you are not doing your

job, we will not correct you from the sideline. We will talk to you on the sideline. We want you to improve individually and as a team as much (if not more) than you do.

Aggressiveness: The game will be won or lost on how we tackle (take the ball from the other team) and on which team gets to the loose ball first. Be there first with your entire body, not just your toe. You will not get hurt if you get your hips over the ball. We must make them react to us, not the other way around.

What Is Next?

If your team has mastered all of these skills early and they have worked well as a team, they are likely to have success on the field. If they are not being challenged much or they just have the itch to move up to another level of play, the next chapter is relevant. Even if you do not think you will ever do elite or travel soccer, it is good to understand what this level entails and what it provides. You may have players move up to a travel team, or your own child might be motivated to play at the elite level. Understandably, you may not want to coach a travel team. It is much different than coaching a house team.

We do not believe that you have to do travel soccer to thoroughly enjoy this wonderful sport. Yet if you do plan to make the transition to travel soccer, the next chapter will provide some frank and practical information.

CHAPTER 6
Moving to Travel Soccer

The shift from house soccer to travel soccer should not be taken lightly. It is important to understand when you might make the move and what you will need to do if you move to travel soccer. In addition, it is useful to understand specifics of indoor soccer, since it is likely that your travel team will participate in some form of indoor soccer.

When to Move

Making the move from house soccer to travel soccer is a large step for both the parents and for the kids playing. It normally costs a lot more money, requires many more time commitments, and needs a lot more volunteers than for a house team.

Therefore, you must ask yourself two questions if your team or a single player on your team is ready for travel:

1. *Are they being challenged in house soccer?* A team can win every game and still be challenged by its opponents. However, if the other teams never score a goal and your players are not improving their individual or team skills, then they probably are not being challenged. You should observe this situation for two or three seasons before you decide to make the move to travel soccer.

2. *Are they losing interest in other sports and want to play only soccer?* Most young boys and girls who play soccer are active and play lots of sports. This is healthy and wise. Playing only one sport all year long at seven or eight years old is bad for the young athlete. It is even questionable for young teenagers. However, you slowly start to see what some kids want

to do as their favorite sport. A very healthy balance is to have soccer as the primary sport in the spring and the fall, but have it be secondary to some other sport in the summer and the winter. My daughter transitioned to travel soccer when she was ten years old but still focused on swimming in the summer and the winter. In the fall and spring soccer was king. This cross-training was good for her young body and provided enough repetitions to permit her to improve her soccer skills and compete at a high level in swimming.

In most soccer clubs, travel teams are permitted to form when the players enter the U9 league. So what does a travel team do that a house team does not? There are basically four major differences:

1. Travel teams have a paid trainer and possibly a paid coach. We highly recommend that you delay having a paid coach for as long as possible. Keep the team run by a parent with the best interest of the players, as children, in mind, and do not confuse it for a developmental league for high school or college programs.

2. Travel teams play in tournaments as a key part of the season. This was the primary reason why I (Darren) originally took my house team to travel. The opportunity to play in a tournament is an exceptional learning experience. The usual four games in a weekend tournament amounts to a month's worth of games in a regular schedule, so the players learn so much in a single tournament. Tournaments can help reinforce good habits and break bad habits.

3. Travel teams need to have parents take on a variety of volunteer positions. The coach cannot do everything, like you might need to do for a house team.

4. Travel teams play much tougher teams, many of which are really serious about soccer. This means that you need to be ready to lose some soccer games. However, even in travel soccer, as long as you continue to focus on learning and improving, your team will do well.

What to Do

If you are going to be the coach for a travel team or join an existing travel team, be aware of the following list of tasks to accomplish. This list will provide you with the proper context to make the transition smoothly and to better understand the time commitment of travel soccer.

1. *Select players.* We suggest selecting the best athletes, not the best soccer players, at this point. You will have years to train soccer, but you cannot coach speed, intensity, good work ethic, and other traits.

2. *Select a team name.* You will keep this team name for a long time, unlike in house leagues, where you normally change your team names at least each year. Look at out-of-state leagues for names that you might want to use. Think about a name that lends itself to an interesting logo, since you may have this on your jerseys, bumper stickers, decals, and more for years. Look on the Web site of the league you will enter to make sure you are not selecting a name that another team in your age group already has. Last, let both the parents and the players be part of the selection process.

3. *Select a league.* Start with the lowest, least-competitive league first. Many travel teams make the mistake of trying to rocket to the top of the soccer world in one year and often get burned out (overworked and overtrained) or demoralized because they do not win any games. Take your time. Win the lowest division in the lowest league, and work your way up.

4. *Select a manager.* The manager for travel teams is critical, since this person handles all of the registration, roster changes, and related matters. You cannot be a good coach and a good manager at the same time, so do not try to do it. This is a time-consuming volunteer job, so make sure whoever volunteers has the time and energy to do it well.

5. *Determine how much money you want to pay.* This is a crucial decision, and it varies from team to team. One approach is to go all out and do everything to increase your chances of winning and look good doing it. This may result in seasonal costs (so they would occur twice a year) of more than $1,000 per player.

However, the only expenditure that really determines how well your team will perform is the trainer. You can normally get a good trainer, pay for basic uniforms, and enter two tournaments a season for a seasonal cost per player below $500. Just as with the league selection, we suggest you start at the low end of the budget spectrum and work your way up consistent with your players' and their parents' desires.

6. *Select a treasurer.* You need someone to handle the financial concerns, such as collecting money from parents, paying team fees, and reimbursing parent volunteers for approved expenditures. As with the manager's job, do not try to do this yourself, or you will do everything poorly. In addition, when it comes to money, it is good to have someone else involved anyway to provide advice and to check numbers.

7. *Select a trainer.* This is the most important decision that a coach has to make in transitioning to travel status, since the trainer is the one who teaches the soccer skills that the youth soccer coach normally does not have. We wrote this book for parents who want to be a soccer coach even though they may have played little to no soccer. So the trainer introduces these coaches and the players to technical aspects of soccer critical to advancing the competency of the team.

Normally, there are many youth soccer training organizations in decent-sized cities, but the best thing to do before hiring a trainer is to talk to other travel coaches. However, be aware that fellow travel coaches likely will not refer you to their trainer, since each trainer has relatively few teams that they can handle. Good trainers are in high demand, so you need to start looking early and investigate every possible lead. Look not only for a primary trainer for your team, but also for a person who might take that trainer's place when he is sick. A great trainer who does not have a quality backup will be a problem during the season, since he invariably will have to miss a practice or two throughout the season.

Most trainers are not full-time trainers; they have a full-time job, just like you. Many work in real estate or mortgage industries or other fields that allow them more flexibility with their hours and commitments.

8. *Select tournaments.* The selection of tournaments depends on the experience of the team. Teams that are just starting travel usually participate in just two tournaments a season, while other teams might enter up to ten a year. Similarly, a team just starting travel soccer might enter only local tournaments, while more advanced teams sometimes travel many states away to play tougher teams. Most states have a soccer association that will provide a list of sanctioned tournaments, which typically cost $400–$600 to register. Once you participate in one or two tournaments, you will be inundated with e-mails and mailings for future tournaments. You will have more to choose from than you have the time or money to do.

9. *Determine if and how you will raise money for the team.* Your team has three primary sources of money: parents, sponsors, and fund-raising. The bulk of the money needed to pay for team expenses (such as uniforms, the trainer, equipment, and tournaments) will come from the parents. A travel soccer team usually has two payments a year ranging from $500 to $1,000.

However, teams frequently supplement the money from parents by either asking for sponsors or doing fund-raising activities. Local businesses such as pizza restaurants, dentist offices, car dealerships, and ice cream parlors might provide $150–$500 each year to have their logo displayed on the team Web site or on the team banner. It is also customary to provide the sponsors with a plaque for their wall thanking them for their sponsorship. This is valuable to the sponsors—visible proof that they are involved in the community. You might also have a sponsor appreciation day, where your sponsors have the opportunity to provide some marketing material to the parents of the team. Other firms sponsor youth soccer teams just to have a tax exemption.

The other source of funds for your soccer team could be fund-raising, such as bake sales and selling wrapping paper or cookie dough. When your local soccer club conducts organizational meetings, they will allow small companies who can assist in fund-raisers to talk with you.

Ultimately, it is up to you and the parents of your players to decide how much you want to spend on your travel soccer team and how much help you would like to receive from sponsors or fund-raisers in paying for it.

10. *Select other volunteers.* Coaching a travel soccer team requires much more help from all the parents of your players. As coach, you must be able to delegate responsibilities. We have already discussed the need for a manager, assistant coach(es), and a treasurer, but the list of other volunteers you should consider include social coordinator, uniform manager, publicity, sponsor coordinator, tournament director (for each tournament), Web site manager, and team photographer. Aim for at least one parent of each player to have some job in supporting the running of the team.

Indoor Soccer

Teams who are in the elite or travel status are usually the ones who participate in indoor soccer. The winter indoor game provides a way for players to keep their soccer skills sharp between the fall and spring soccer seasons. If you are lucky, your team will play on an indoor field with Astroturf, where the kids can continue to wear their soccer cleats during the indoor season. However, many localities do not have that luxury, so you will play on a surface similar to basketball courts or in-line hockey rinks.

No matter where you play, the first thing that you will notice about indoor soccer is that it is a completely different game than outdoor soccer. Indoor is faster, rougher, and requires better ball control and defensive skills. Due to the much smaller field sizes, the games are usually 5v5 or 6v6, even for the older tween teams.

We are not big fans of indoor soccer. It teaches lots of bad habits and creates a dynamic that does not reinforce the skills that we have focused on throughout this book. However, due to the climate of many places around the world and the great demand for outside fields for other sports, you will likely have to participate in indoor soccer if your team or child plays travel soccer. Try to play in an indoor league that does not have sidewalls, since that is closer to the real game of soccer. This type of indoor league is often called *futsol*. When your team plays indoor soccer on a field with walls, it is like playing hockey without sticks.

The tips below are useful for the team just starting indoor soccer. They will help the players adjust to the different pace and spacing when playing on walled fields.

Mark up on defense

Playing defense happens anytime the other team has the ball in your half of the field. As mentioned for outdoor soccer, marking up becomes more important as the quality of the teams you play gets better and better. For sure, when the ball is in your end of the field, your players must mark up someone. Ideally, though, your players will find an opponent to cover as soon as the other team takes possession of the ball.

No matter what position your kids are playing, each is responsible for one opponent. Focusing on defense ensures that they will get the ball back as soon as possible. When your team has the ball, you want them to distance themselves from the other team. However, as soon as the opponent regains the ball, you want each of your players to stick to one player on the other team to make it difficult for them to retain possession. Indoor fields are so small it is almost like playing an entire game within the two 18 yard lines on a regular outdoor soccer field.

Do not let your players "play" goalkeeper unless they have gloves on. Hanging around the goalkeeper does not help. Instruct your players to find a player from the other team and be a pest. For example, if the left fullback has no one behind him but there is an opponent in front of the goal, the fullback should go pester that player.

No double-team on the wall

Do not double-team the ball on the wall. Remember that we discussed trusting one's teammate and not going after the ball if another teammate is already fighting for it. This principle is even more important in indoor soccer, because when the ball pops out of a pileup, which it eventually will, your team will have a player out of position if he is double-teaming the ball. By the way, having two players in the pile fighting for the ball does not double your chances of winning it.

Teach your players to hang out about five to ten feet away and wait to get the ball that pops out, attack the opponent who wins the ball, or receive a pass from the teammate who just won the ball. If the ball is getting plastered against the wall in your end, then your players should stay really close. But make sure that if the opponent has two teammates in the pileup, then you have only two. If you have more than two, then the uncovered opponent likely will be standing in front of your goal by himself!

Continue to remind your players that they should spread out on offense. When they do not have the ball, encourage them to move to an open space where they have a good shot at the goal.

Overplay the wall on transition

When the opposition is dribbling near the wall toward your goal, they likely will use the wall if your players allow it. The wall is a perfect teammate, since it always passes right back and never makes a bad pass. We suggest that you have your players overplay the wall by putting their foot on the edge of the wall, so there is no way that the opponent can pass around your player by using the wall. When the opposition commits to going on the other side of your player, which should be to the middle of the field, your player should push off the wall and challenge the opponent. Make that player pass to a teammate, who should have one of your other players marking up on him, or take the ball from him. If your player forces the opponent to the inside, he will be forced to beat your team one-on-one or make some good passes without the benefit of the wall. Your team will win most of those encounters.

Overplaying the wall is useless for the outdoor game, but it does show you which of your players are more coachable. It may also help you see which teaching techniques work best for other, more universally relevant, soccer skills. Always look for that silver lining and focus on your ability to teach your team, not just whether they win. Eventually, their ability to listen and learn new skills will be the difference between winning and losing.

Shoot the ball

Your team must take lots of shots on goal. It may seem far away, but your players need to take a shot anytime they have the ball in the opponent's half of the field. Teammates must be ready to get the rebound or deflect the ball into the goal.

Once the ball gets down near your opponent's goal, your team needs to be aggressive about getting the ball, but, as stated above, they should not all go to the ball. The closest person should go for the ball and the next closest needs to anticipate where the ball is likely to pop out. This is the pressure and cover defense discussed earlier for outdoor soccer.

Trap and receive the ball softly

This skill takes time and lots of practice to get correct. You must emphasize to your players the importance of trapping the ball with the first touch and not letting it bound away. Your team might be great on the full field outside, pushing the ball hard up a field where there is a lot of space to outrun and outhustle the other team. However, in indoor soccer they need to control the ball and not just send it down the field.

While some skills used in indoor soccer are unnecessary in the outdoor game, the soft touch is amplified and relevant for outdoor soccer. The inability of a player to softly receive a pass will be magnified in indoor soccer since the opponents are so close. Honing this skill is a major motivator for having your team play indoor soccer.

Crisp passing and spacing is a must

This is not kickball. Your players must have some idea what they are going to do with the ball before they start flailing away. Kicking the ball hard is great, but it does no good if the ball goes right back to the opposition. On the smaller fields typical of indoor soccer, a hard-kicked ball often bounds right back to the one who kicked it.

When your players have the ball or are fighting for possession, they should automatically think three things:
1. Am I going to pass it and if so, where?
2. Am I going to dribble the ball around my opponent?
3. Am I going to shoot it?

Think and talk! Figuring out what to do requires that your players know where their teammates are and anticipate where they will go.

If one of your players does not have the ball, he should be moving to open space on offense or marking up on defense. Spacing is important. If your players are all clumped together or strung out across the field in a straight line, there are no passing angles available. Remember the triangle!

What Is Next?

We hope that this book has provided you with some useful ideas about being a youth soccer coach, even if you have never coached before. Do not be afraid. Soccer is an elegantly simple game, and almost anyone can coach the basic aspects (skills, positioning, and stamina). The keys to coaching house soccer in the five-to twelve-year age range are communication, enthusiasm, creativity, and organization.

Good luck, have fun, and help the children on your team learn the wonderful feeling of doing their best every time they get on the field. Do not worry about winning games. Hard work and applying innovatively simple coaching techniques will give you the greatest possible edge in building a successful team. The wins will come without pursuing them as your primary objective, so be patient.

Appendix

This appendix includes several documents that illustrate the type of communication you must have with your players and parents. These show how you need to manage the expectations of your parents and players and provide details of how to run your team. These materials can help you make each season more successful than the last.

- Winter Soccer Homework Sheet: specific weekly homework assignments between the fall and spring seasons.

- BLAST Winter Discussion: a midyear communiqué to team members.

- BLAST Skills Improvement Needs: insights provided to the team trainer to prepare for spring training sessions.

- BLAST Summer Fitness Program: a sheet to tally aerobic workouts during the summer to encourage players staying in shape.

Winter Soccer Homework Sheet

Week Starting 8 Jan	Done?	Week Starting 15 Jan	Done?	Week Starting 22 Jan	Done?	Week Starting 29 Jan	Done
Assignment: Punt ball straight up but back to you about eye level and catch it. This is called volleying. Alternate every ten hits to your other foot. Keep foot pointed. Do as many in a row as possible. Do for five minutes each day.		Assignment: Punt ball straight up **twice** per foot back to you to about eye level and catch it. Keep foot pointed and alternate every six to eight hits. Do for five minutes each day.		Assignment: Punt ball straight up **twice** per foot back to you, then head it to a partner. Do for five minutes each day.		Assignment: Drop the ball on your left thigh and then juggle back to eye level. Alternate legs and see if you can go from left to right as many times as possible. Do for five minutes each day.	
Mon		Mon		Mon		Mon	
Tue		Tue		Tue		Tue	
Wed		Wed		Wed		Wed	
Thu		Thu		Thu		Thu	
Fri		Fri		Fri		Fri	
Sat		Sat		Sat		Sat	
Sun		Sun		Sun		Sun	

Week Starting 5 Feb	Done?	Week Starting 12 Feb	Done?	Week Starting 19 Feb	Done?	Week Starting 26 Feb	Done
Assignment: Roll the ball around the house wherever you go (except the stairs). Push it back and forth while you are doing your homework, eating dinner, etc. Do not kick it in the house! Do this at least one hour each day.		Assignment: Drop the ball on your left thigh and then juggle back to eye level. Alternate legs and see if you can go from left to right as many times as possible. Do for five minutes each day.		Assignment: Combine volleying with your feet with juggling on your thighs. Try to throw in a header whenever possible. Do for five minutes each day.		Assignment: Roll the ball around the house wherever you go (except the stairs). Push it back and forth while you are doing your homework, eating dinner, etc. Do not kick it in the house! Do this at least one hour each day.	
Mon		Mon		Mon		Mon	
Tue		Tue		Tue		Tue	
Wed		Wed		Wed		Wed	
Thu		Thu		Thu		Thu	
Fri		Fri		Fri		Fri	
Sat		Sat		Sat		Sat	
Sun		Sun		Sun		Sun	

BLAST Winter Discussion

The BLAST had a great season.

- The only two goals scored on the winner of our division were scored by the BLAST.
- First season in travel most teams do not win any games. We won three!
- BLAST never lost by more than two goals and most losses were only one goal.
- Tournament performance was exceptional: three goals for and six goals against, lost to eventual champion by closest margin of any other team.
- One third of the players on the team were new and only two girls had travel experience before the season began.
- Your coaches are engineers and scientists. Yikes!

Everybody helped this season.

- Hannah's Dad—Bob as assistant coach leading speed and agility camps.
- Alli's Dad—Dean as manager: lots to learn starting a new travel team and stayed action-packed all season long.
- Alli's Mom—Kathy as activities co-coordinator and sometimes stand-in manager.
- Emily's Dad—Sean as photographer, assistant coach, and organizer for winter indoor program.
- Grace's Mom—Alison as uniform coordinator and sponsor plaques plus dealing with the coach.
- Jen's Dad—Eric as treasurer and occasional assistant coaching duties.
- Jen's Mom—Lori bringing Hamisi to help with the team.
- Katie's Mom—Sue as assistant coach
- Devin's Mom—Suzanne has been working hard to get sponsors and has brought great insights to the coaches from Devin's travel soccer experiences.
- Brianne's Mom—Lisa as the grand organizer of tournaments.
- Danielle's Mom—Susie made the great personalized hair twisties for the girls.

- Danielle's Dad—Steve is getting us sponsors.
- Lacy's Mom—Cammy did the great soccer cards for the sponsors.
- Lacy's Dad—Derek took great pictures and got a sponsor.
- Cori's Mom—Marnie organized our ill-fated first tournament last season.
- Jessie's Mom—Barb got the banner made for us, along with the sponsor logos, and even puts it up every game.
- Brianna's Mom—Sandy made those great photo buttons of the girls and also was activities co-coordinator with Kathy.
- Jordan's Dad—David was the goalkeeper coach extraordinaire, fielded the best Web site in the ODSL, and is helping to coordinate the winter program.
- Every parent has been a chauffeur and medic all season. Thanks!

Here is what we learned this past season.

- *Travel soccer is different than house soccer.* 1. Your daughter must really want to be playing soccer for *both* practice and the games ("Mom, can I go to practice early?" or, "Darn, practice was cancelled!"). 2. Your daughter must really want to learn from the coaches, trainers, and each other. 3. Our three basics are even more important than before: thinking, hustling, and what they do without the ball. 4. Focus must be on soccer during the fall and spring seasons (second only to church, family, and school). 5. Practice is important. You do not have skills during the game if you do not work hard in practice. Practice makes permanent, not perfect. *Winter soccer will be expected next year,* and every girl should take some soccer training over the summer in addition to the BLAST summer camp slated for the last two weeks of the summer. The girls need the reps. 6. We need to examine getting more and different trainer support. Next fall it may make sense to have a trainer twice a week. Eventually, many teams also have a paid coach.

- *Attitude is #1.* We will not put up with an attitude that anyone on the team is a star or they do not need to hustle all of the time. If I have a problem, I will let you know. At this age, attitude is just as important as skill, smarts, or speed. The girls should be having fun and enjoying soccer. Coaches and parents also need to control themselves in bugging the referees about rough plays and bad calls. Being a referee is tough and hounding the referee will not help us get any close calls. It also makes us look bad. I will talk to the referees quietly and discretely either at halftime or after the game if there is a problem.

- *Soccer is a beautiful sport.* Some of the passes, crosses, shots, tackles, saves, etc., by the BLAST this last season were works of art. We see great things for the BLAST if we continue to work and focus on getting better and really *learning and enjoying the sport,* not just *playing the game.* I will strive to continue to get the best trainer for our girls and bring in guest trainers to get some variety of ideas about soccer. The coaches will work hard to get smarter about all aspects of the game: conditioning, stretching, offensive schemes, drills, communications, etc. The coaches will be giving directions less *from the sideline* and coaching more *on the sideline.* Consistency of coaching will also be emphasized.

We still need to be looking for more sponsors in the off-season.

- More sponsors means paying less over time or getting more items to support the team.
- For every sponsor who pays $250, each family pays about $20 less.
- Fee per family of $425 for the spring (same as the fall): expenses are $1,100 for tournaments, $650 for registration, $1,100 for training in March, and $1,750 for trainer in spring. Maybe a pop-up bench? Please hand or mail $425 check to Darren or Eric by February 10.

What to expect in the spring.

- Bob will start the speed and agility camps as soon as possible.
- Start practice on March 1, even though the regular season does not start until April 1. We will have trainers during March to examine potential alternatives for next year.
- Tuesday and Thursday (at Rocky Run from 5:00 to6:30 PM). The Tuesdays will be the trainer days. They even will give us a bonus session on Tuesday, February 27, if the weather is good enough.
- Every Sunday (March 4, 11, 18) from 3:00 to5:00 PM at EDS with Hamisi.
- We will ask for a bye on spring break and there are no games for Easter weekend.
- I do not know what fields we will get for practice yet, but I will clearly try to keep them the same as this last season, if at all possible.
- We will plan on attending at least two tournaments: We need tournament directors again. I have already registered us for the March tournament

below. Please let me know which tournament would be best for you in May. We are leaning toward the local one over the holiday weekend rather than driving to Blacksburg!

March 24–25, 2007, PWSI ICEBREAKER. Hosted by **Prince William Soccer Inc. (North).** Entry fee for U9–U11 is $475. Entry deadline is February 20, 2007. **Club Teams** with up to four guest players for U9–U12. The tournament is accepting boys and girls teams.

May 19–20, 2007, NEW RIVER UNITED SOCCER/VIRGINIA TECH SUMMER KICKOFF. Hosted by **New River United Soccer (West).** Entry fee for U11–U14 is $425. Entry deadline is April 20, 2007. **Club Teams** with up to five guest players. The tournament is accepting boys and girls teams.

OR

May 26–27, 2007, VIRGINIAN SOCCER TOURNAMENT. Hosted by **Springfield Youth Club (North).** Entry fee is $595 for U9–U10, $650 for U11–U16, and $700 for U17–U19. Entry deadline is April 16, 2007. **Club Teams** with up to three guest players for all age groups. The tournament is accepting boys and girls teams.

• A few minor adjustments to positions and rotations will be made in March using professional trainers to help in assessments.

I think that the girls will make a quantum leap in skills and results this next season. We want to provide an environment where everyone is challenged but still has fun.

Coach D

BLAST Skills Improvement Needs

Defensive and Transition: Mostly Physical Play (Play Hard)

Possession. Help girls to get and then maintain the ball under their hips. Defend against opponents by keeping their hips above the ball and blocking out their opponent. This includes dribbling the ball under pressure both downfield and laterally (side to side). This also includes *soft feet* in receiving passes/ trapping air balls and maintaining possession on throw-ins.

Marking up on defense. Do not give the other team the chance to have clean, uncontested shots in our 18 yard line. Move to opponents naturally as they approach our 18 yard line, not just *to* them but *on* them.

Offensive: Mostly Rapid Decision Making and Timing (Play Smart)

Accurate and timely passing. I want them to work on making precise passes and knowing when to dribble versus when to pass. This includes anticipating better on offense, passing to the open area (the girl with the ball), and anticipating the pass to the open area and beating the defender to it (the girl receiving the ball).

Quick and hard shooting. We should be a threat anytime we get the ball cleanly in their 18 yard line. This means shooting with your left foot, since sometimes to get a quick shot you will have to shoot with the left foot. This includes a stronger corner kick set play, where you kick into the playing area and offensive players' response to this kick being better timed.

The BLAST is pretty good at spacing, positioning, hustling, and filling the lanes on defense, defensive rotation, and angles against advancing players with the ball. However, please have the girls work on whatever you think will enable them to be more competitive in travel soccer. We never lost by more than one goal, but we also never scored more than three goals, so we are decidedly too defensive and lack explosive offensive capability.

BLAST Summer Fitness Program

The intent of this program is to ensure that you do not get out of shape over the summer. I know that for most of you this will not be necessary, but it is important to not allow getting in shape in September to detract from the soccer skills that we will be working on.

Please make a check mark next to each day below. The goal is to have a check mark at least five days a week during the summer. You earn a check mark by:

- Biking for more than 60 minutes.
- Walking for more than 50 minutes.
- Swimming for more than 40 minutes; any swim team practice or a meet where you swim three or more events, including the IM, counts.
- Running or doing the elliptical trainer for more than 30 minutes.
- Any comparable activity that breaks a sweat and lasts for more than 30 minutes. For example, a 3-hour soccer session, a speed and agility session with Coach Bob, or rock climbing on a cruise ship in the Caribbean would all count.

Do not forget to stretch *after* any of these activities! I do not want anybody running more than three days a week, and never run two days in a row. It is too much pounding.

There will be awards given during the August BLAST Camp for most consistent, most imaginative ways to get credit, activity farthest from home to get credit, etc.

July	?	July	?	July	?	July	?	July	?
1		8		15		22		29	
2		9		16		23		30	
3		10		17		24		31	
4		11		18		25		Aug 1	
5		12		19		26		2	
6		13		20		27		3	
7		14		21		28		4	

Aug	?	Aug	?	Aug	?
5		12		19	
6		13		20	
7		14		21	
8		15		22	
9		16		23	
10		17		24	
11		18		25	

Player Name: _____

978-0-595-46787-7
0-595-46787-3

23107079R00111

Made in the USA
Lexington, KY
27 May 2013